Torah Without End

Neo-Hasidic Torah and Practices in Honor of Rabbi Jonathan Slater

Edited by Rabbi Michael Strassfeld

Ben Yehuda Press
Teaneck, New Jersey

Published by Ben Yehuda Press
122 Ayers Court #1B
Teaneck, NJ 07666

http://www.BenYehudaPress.com

To subscribe to our monthly book club and support independent Jewish publishing, visit https://www.patreon.com/BenYehudaPress

Ben Yehuda Press books may be purchased at a discount by synagogues, book clubs, and other institutions buying in bulk.
For information, please email markets@BenYehudaPress.com

ISBN13 978-1-953829-41-2

22 23 24 / 10 9 8 7 6 5 4 3 2 1   202211123

Contents

Foreword
What Is Spirituality?

Josh Feigelson

משנה אבות ד':ו'
רַבִּי יוֹסֵי אוֹמֵר, כָּל הַמְכַבֵּד אֶת הַתּוֹרָה, גּוּפוֹ מְכֻבָּד עַל הַבְּרִיּוֹת.
וְכָל הַמְחַלֵּל אֶת הַתּוֹרָה, גּוּפוֹ מְחֻלָּל עַל הַבְּרִיּוֹת.

Rabbi Yose said: whoever honors the Torah is themselves honored by others, and whoever dishonors the Torah is themselves dishonored by others. (Avot 4:6)

What does it mean to honor Torah? Commenting on Rabbi Yose's statement in the Mishnah, Maimonides teaches that "honor of the Torah is [manifested] in teaching alacrity in its performance and honoring the sages that support it and the books they wrote about it" (Commentary on the Mishnah, *ad loc*). According to the Rambam, to honor the Torah is to create a field of *kavod* around it: It involves not only performing the Torah's mitzvot energetically, but, even more so, cultivating teachers and teachings in relation to it. *K'vod haTorah*, honor of the Torah, is thus ultimately about teaching Torah, writing Torah, and nurturing an ongoing and living relationship between the Jewish people and its ever-renewing textual inheritance.

But there is more. If we stopped only with Maimonides's explanation, we might understand *k'vod haTorah* to be a kind of hard-edged, formalistic relationship with authority: We honor the Torah by standing up in its presence and in the presence of those who teach it; we assign the Torah and its scholars a certain authoritative weight. But what about our own inner life? How is *k'vod haTorah* manifest in the inner chambers of our hearts and minds?

The early hasidic master R' Israel Hopstein, known as the Maggid of Kozhnitz, helps us go further. "The intention here is to say that honoring the Torah is when one realizes that Torah is not an empty vessel—but rather that in every word and letter and jot there are great mysteries and secrets," he writes. "When one studies Torah with this awareness and with intention toward this inner experience, and with the complete faith that every word of Torah she has studied is full of deeper meanings, and thus connects the Torah she is studying with the Torah that exists in the supernal realms—this is the honor of the Torah" *(Avodat Yisrael, ad loc.)*

For the Maggid, the term *kavod* connotes not only a field of honor or prestige around the Torah, but an embodied physical connection, a presence, between the individual(s) engaged in study, those who came before them, and the Divine who speaks in and through the text. In classic Hasidic fashion, he finds meaning in a seemingly throwaway word in the Mishnah: גופו, *gufo.* In the original Mishnaic context, the word simply means "he." But in a literal sense, *gufo* means "his body," and thus the Maggid renders the Mishnah as saying not only that one who honors the Torah will be honored among people, but, in a sense both deeper and even more literal, "his body will be connected by means of his soul upwards to *Ein Sof,* and the light of his soul will illuminate his body." That is, Torah study has the capacity to light up not only our minds, but our souls and our bodies as well.

This is the kind of Torah study Jonathan Slater has helped me and an entire generation of rabbis, cantors, and laypeople to discover—a Torah that is not only intellectually stimulating, rigorous, and erudite, but that activates our hearts and bodies as much as our intellects. While Torah can always be "interesting," Jonathan invites us and challenges us to ask the vital question that moves Torah beyond merely being interesting to becoming transformative: How, if at all, is this text true in your own experience? What, if anything, could it mean for you? What might it awaken in your inner life? How might you go further in your understanding of the text?

Jonathan has done that through his own writing and teaching, and, equally important, through raising up and supporting many more writers and teachers of Torah (myself included). Those of us fortunate enough to have worked with Jonathan as our editor through the IJS text study program have experienced how Jonathan gently pushes and prods as he helps us expand our own awareness of the possibilities for meaning in the text—and the possibilities for engaging our readers and learners in their own experience of deeper and more expansive meaning. In doing so, he has embodied not only the Maggid of Kozhnitz's understanding of *k'vod haTorah,* but also that of the Rambam. He has plowed and sewn a field of scholar-practitioners, cultivated and tended it, and witnessed its flourishing.

With my own academic scholar cap on, I have long observed that, perhaps more than anything else, what defines the liberal Jewish community in America is higher education and the values of the academy. We are now well into the third generation in which the overwhelming majority of liberal Jews attend college. One of the results of this phenomenon is that the liberal Jewish community has taken on the approach to knowledge and study that dominates academic life, characterized by objectivity and detachment. That is all well and good, but it has come at a cost, particularly as those values have come to color many Jews' relationship with Torah.

The Maggid, perhaps responding to the Enlightenment around him, concludes his comment on our Mishnah with an observation on its second half:

> *One who desecrates* (מחלל) *the Torah:* That is who makes the Torah hollow (חלול), drained of vitality, and simply a book of stories, not filled with mysteries and depths... In this one's thought, there is no inner life to the Torah... To this one, the Torah is like a body without a soul, and thus this one does not draw forth the inner vitality—the soulful depths we have discussed above. And thus, this one's own physical body is likewise hollow; that is, they are made hollow as they have detached their soul.

Historicism, empiricism, science: these are all vital and important tools of knowledge. But, as we have learned through our own experience, the move to objectivity, if unaccompanied by a robust engagement with our subjectivity—with our lived experience and inner life—can lead to the withering of our relationship with Torah, a hollowing out and detachment that has ultimately left too many untethered from their own Jewishness.

This, it seems to me, is what so many people in the late 20th and early 21st centuries have sought: an approach to Torah that is at once intellectually honest and rigorous and, simultaneously, engages our bodies and souls. And this is precisely the Torah that Jonathan Slater has developed and nurtured with immense intelligence, skill, and, most importantly, love. Jonathan has helped many thousands of Jews rediscover, restore, rehabilitate, and renew their relationship with Torah. He has raised up a generation of students who continue to plow the field and expand it, finding new insights and expressions of Torah and helping ever-increasing numbers to relate to it fully—in mind, body, and spirit. There can be no greater expression of the meaning of *k'vod haTorah* than that.

Rabbi Josh Feigelson is President & CEO of the Institute for Jewish Spirituality.

Bereshit
Bridging the Gap between the Upper and Lower Worlds

Moshe Re'em

What is spirituality? Martin Buber distinguished "religiosity" from "religion." For Buber, religiosity describes the human "urge to establish a living communion with the unconditioned." It is the human "will to realize the unconditioned through deed, and to establish it in the world" (*On Judaism*, p. 93). Buber's concept of "religiosity" comes close to what one may consider "spirituality." It transcends the particularity of religion. In hasidic terms, while spirituality (*ruchaniyut*) belongs to the "upper world," the institution of religion is rooted in the lower world of *gashmiyut*. The aim of "spirituality" is to transform the institutionalized *gashmiyut* of religion, thereby unifying the lower and upper worlds.

Levi Yitzhak suggests one way to accomplish this through Shabbat. In Kedushat Levi, in commenting on the verse, "On it (the seventh day), God rested (*shavat*) from all God's work that God created and made" (Genesis 2:3) he writes: "Understand the phrase 'On it, mei God rested (*shavat*),' from the Hebrew verb 'return,' *chazarah*, (Levi Yitzhak is linking the Hebrew word *shavat* to the root *shuv*, 'return'). "Through human actions in the lower world (on earth), a person can transcend and rise to the higher world." The holiness of Shabbat lies in its potential to serve as a transformative experience, a sort of portal to the higher world.

Humans (*adam*) who are, by nature, deeply rooted in the material world (*adamah*), including its religious institutions, can use Shabbat as a way to experience *ruchaniyut*. Shabbat more than any other day of the week has the potential to connect us with the Transcendent. It is infused, as it were, with part of that *ruach Elohim* that exists in the creation of the lower world.

The practice of mindful walking on Shabbat, whether to shul or an afternoon *shpatzir*, can serve as a way of freeing us from the fetters of the material world, even as our feet are grounded in the lower world. Focus your *CHI* downward toward the earth, even as your breath raises your consciousness to a higher realm.

As a spiritual practice, Shabbat transforms institutionalized religion into a more spiritual experience. It can serve as a means to connect us to something more transcendent. But we need to constantly work at it. We need to reset that intention again and again, on a weekly basis. It is our good fortune that Shabbat was created as a *mei-ain olam ha-ba*, "a foretaste of the World to Come," in order to facilitate *ma-on olam ha-elyon*, "our dwelling in the upper world," if only we will it, if only for a moment, if only for this moment.

Rabbi Moshe Re'em lives in Allentown, Pa. He was in the 5th cohort of the Institute's Rabbinic Leadership Program and has participated in Hevraya retreats.

Jonathan's love for Levi Yitzhak is infectious. His teaching, sensitivity and insights have served as a constant inspiration for how to utilize the teachings of classical Hasidic thought in ways to inform and transform our experience of the holy.

Noah
These are the generations of Noah...make for yourself an ark of gopher wood...

Myriam Klotz

Concerning the ark, the Blessed God gave Noah advice and protection until the days of wrath would pass, and similarly all whose hearts are still restless can receive advice from the ark as to how to find refuge from all the evil that unsettles the world. This we find in the words of our sages (*Tanna Dvei Eliyahu Rabba*, Chapter 6): "If someone sees that suffering comes upon themselves, they are to run to the inner chambers of the Torah, and it will give them advice as to how to survive.' The matter of the ark has to do with what is written in the Gemara (Pesahim 113b), 'There are three whom the Blessed Holy One loves—one who does not get angry, one who does not get drunk, and one who forgives.'"
—*Mei HaShiloach* (Rabbi Mordechai Yoseph of Izbica)

What is it about these three qualities that the *Mei HaShiloach* connects to the sense of refuge that the ark provides to Noah, and to any of us whose hearts are restless in unsettled times?

First, let's clarify what the ark here represents. To build an ark is literally to build a refuge, a structure within which physical life can be protected and preserved amidst even the most catastrophic floods of life.

What about the inner life? To build an inner ark is to create an inner structure through practice that cultivates life-giving awareness and clear-seeing.

When the body is agitated and emotions are triggered, an inner life built through devoted spiritual practice can be our refuge. We can turn to the depth teaching of the Torah to ease our hearts and guide our actions, and to bring us comfort and hope.

There are three ways of acting that are especially loved by God in the ark— we can understand these characteristics to be fruits of practice:

How do we work with anger when it arises within us? See it, be aware of it, work with it internally before reacting externally so that whatever actions are taken are grounded in awareness and love.

Second, how do we stay present when we feel aversion or desire, when we'd rather avoid facing the difficulties surrounding us? The practice offered for refuge here is to "not get drunk." The *Mei HaShiloach* says that sobriety represents a settled mind, a state of balance that can better ride the waves of desire and aversion. Clarity is rooted in awareness of the interdependence of all life.

Third, we can find refuge in the practice of forgiveness. The ark is built to withstand the karmic consequences of humanity's foibles and sins. We will continue to harm and be harmed in this life because we are not perfect, and we don't always get it right. In learning to forgive ourselves and others, we enter into the heart of Torah: forgive, and incline towards love. It is in cultivating a heart capable of forgiveness (and this is a lifelong practice), that we can find inner refuge and *No'ach*, the repose and rest, reflected in Noah's name.

Mindfulness meditation, prayer, spiritual direction, study, yoga and other somatic practices are among the spiritual practices you can work with to build up your inner "ark". An interior resilience and awareness can sustain you and provide guidance for wise action during difficult times. May this be so in your life, and in all the generations yet to be.

Rabbi Myriam Klotz (she/they) is a Senior Program Director at the Institute for Jewish Spirituality. Myriam loves and appreciates Jonathan's steadfast capacity to "hold the pose" in practice and life.

Lekh Lekha
Go to Your Sacred Source

Lisa Gelber

At age ten, I knew I wanted to be a rabbi. My dream was filled with obstacles and unknowns.

A deep connection with Jewish tradition that did not articulate a central place for me as a woman at the time and place in which I was raised.

The joy of practice that placed me in the chain of tradition and left me hanging on an open clasp.

The relationship to God taught as something foreign from how I now engage with the holy and sacred.

Looking back, I think I knew in my core how I wanted to manifest in the world even if I did not yet have the words for that call. Perhaps this is why I see Avram's call as a powerful expression of authenticity, a journey of magnetic internal force.

ויאמר ה אל אברם

The Holy One said to Avram

לך לך

You, go!

מארצך

From your land

וממולדתך

From the place you were born

ומבית אביך

And from your father's house

אל הארץ אשר אראך

To the land that I will show you

What is this land? Where is this place that takes us from what seeded and grew us? This journey is about who we are on the inside and how we are called to be in this world. R. Levi Yitzhak of Berdichev sees this clearly. He comments on Genesis 12:1, "This is a fundamental lesson. Wherever you go, you are going to your rooted place... That is what God meant in saying 'Go forth (*lekh lekha*)'. "Go...to your source, and there raise up those sparks." Life is a journey towards the essence of who we are, the core that holds us upright as a human created in God's image. This is the place from which we raise up the sparks of our unique self. This is the energy and focus connected to our root soul, the source of our being.

Don't be afraid to dig deep and connect with the genuine place from which the blessings of imagination and fortitude emerge. Come to know yourself and raise up your holy sparks.

Practice:

Connect with your root source by making a gentle fist with one hand and placing it on your sternum. Take a deep breath in, and then exhale. Gently pull your shoulders back. Take a deep breath in, and then exhale. Extend the fingers of your other hand over your fist, letting the cradled hands rest against your chest. Take a deep breath in, and then exhale. Continue to breathe in and out, letting the breath circle through your heart and awaken your *kishkes*. Be present in this posture, standing or sitting, and feel your sparks fly.

Rabbi Lisa Gelber is rabbi, mother, marathon runner, spiritual director, breast cancer survivor and Peloton enthusiast. She lives, writes, runs and spins in NYC with her Torah muse and daughter, Zahara.

Lisa expresses abundant gratitude to Jonathan for honoring the sacred source in each of us and amplifying our sparks.

Vayeira
Seeking Your Presence Through the Day

Ruth H. Sohn

Parashat Vayeira opens with God appearing to Abraham, who is sitting at the entrance to his tent in the heat of the day (Genesis 18:1). Looking up, Abraham sees three men standing before him. What follows is the well-known story that captures so well Abraham's eagerness to welcome and offer hospitality to strangers. Abraham runs forward to greet the three men, and bowing to the ground, says *"Adonai, my lords, please don't pass by..."* offering them rest and refreshment.

Perhaps the best-known lesson drawn from the timing of Abraham's dramatic offer of hospitality is that extending hospitality to others is even more important than our connecting with the Divine (Shabbat 127b).

But what if this narrative is saying something different? According to the Hasidic Master, the *Me'or Einayim*, Abraham was initially speaking to God, not the men standing before him. This adds a whole new dimension to Abraham's words: *"Adonai,* Living Presence (lit: My Lord), if I have found favor in Your sight, please don't pass by Your servant..." —saying in effect: "My God, even as I now turn to welcome these passersby, may I remain attached to You."

How often do we long for greater connection between those moments of deep awareness of Divine Presence and "the rest of our lives"—that is, the more "ordinary" moments as we encounter different people and tasks through the day, even as some of these involve the fulfillment of *mitzvot?*

The *Me'or Einayim's* reading of our verses points us to spiritual practices that might support a more sustained connection to an expansive, loving Presence through the day.

What if, as we come to the close of prayer or meditation, we were to turn to the Infinite Loving Presence, as did Abraham, and say: "Infinite Presence, as I turn now to step into my day and to engage with the people and tasks before me, please stay with me... help me continue to feel Your Presence and Your love, and to be guided by Your Light."

During the day, can we look for moments to pause, and for just a breath or two, to dwell at the entrance of our tent—the space between this moment and the next? As we take a breath, let's notice and welcome whatever sensations are arising in our body, inviting the release of any tension we might be holding. With a breath or two, might we be able to open again to the expansiveness of Infinite Loving Presence? And can we ask God's help in bringing this sense of Divine Presence with us into the next task before us?

With a sustained or renewed sense of Loving Presence through the day, may we be better able to see and hear from an open heart and to respond with greater compassion and clarity.

Rabbi Ruth H. Sohn, a rabbi, teacher, writer and spiritual companion, was in the original IJS rabbinic cohort with Jonathan. She deeply appreciates Jonathan's love of and expansive understanding of Hasidic texts and their sources in earlier Jewish rabbinic and Zoharic traditions, and his tremendous generosity of spirit as a teacher, colleague, and human being.

Chayyei Sarah
The Perfect Union

Lydia Medwin

There is something so poetic about the fact that we learn about the death of both Abraham and Sarah in the same parashah. Partners as they were in life, they are also paralleled in death, not only because of the location in our weekly Torah reading cycle, but also in the commentary that remarks on the way their deaths are described. Sarah dies and, as the only woman in Torah whose age is mentioned, the Torah reports the length of her life by hundreds of years, tens of years, and ones of years.

Rashi notes that "years" was repeatedly mentioned in this way to indicate Sarah's dedication, year in and year out, in every season of her life, to doing good deeds. As Abraham approaches his own death and his years are enumerated, the Torah uses an uncommon formulation: *ba b'yamim*, "he comes with his days." The *Sefat Emet* comments that Abraham was imbued with the gift of remembering everything he learned, of bringing his learning with him every day as if it were as fresh and wondrous as the day he first learned it.

Taken together, the description of Abraham and Sarah's years pair well in describing the dynamic two-part dance of mindfulness practice at its best. Abraham teaches us about the awakening and insight that mindfulness affords us. Even as forgetfulness forever pulls us towards worldliness and materialism, an awakened mind sees the world as it is: continually renewed, engaging us in its marvelous and enduring unfolding. We can *ba b'yamim*, bring each day to awareness, when we remember that the everyday "stuff" is actually the stuff of miracles.

Sarah brings the second half of the dance, the one where we figure out how to live this wonder out into our lives, into the world, and for the benefit of others. Mindfulness practice is, at its root, not only about self-discovery or self-improvement. It can only reach its fullest potential as a powerful spiritual tool when our awe of God turns into reverence for all human life, when our inner goodness spills over into acts of goodness. We are emulating Sarah when our practice helps us bring more peace, more justice, and more wholeness to the families and communities with whom we live.

Therefore, this is the practice of the pair, Abraham and Sarah: Breath in Abraham, and become awake to this moment. Breath out Sarah, and make a commitment to a physical expression of justice and peace. Breath in, and become aware of the wondrous renewal of creation. Breath out, and become aware of our responsibilities as partners in that creation. Breath in, and see reality as it is, right now. Breath out, and envision reality as it could be, as it should be. Then, get up off the cushion, and make it real.

Rabbi Lydia Medwin is an associate rabbi at The Temple in Atlanta, GA. Jonathan is precious to her as the one who challenged her to find God in justice work and share that Presence with her community just as much as we would in the midst of prayer.

Toldot
The Forgotten Blessing

Nancy Kasten

Esau gets a bad rap in Jewish tradition. After all, Jacob only gets top billing in the pantheon of Jewish ancestry because he cheated his older brother out of his rightful place. You can't really blame Esau for being upset and resentful. In fact, we might feel compassion for someone in his position who says to himself, in the heat of the moment, "I'm going to kill that fraudster when our father is gone." We might also admire his restraint—-if he really intended to murder Jacob, he didn't have to wait.

From a mindfulness perspective, Esau deserves a lot of credit for making his father (and us) think more expansively about what "blessing" can mean. The *Sefat Emet* (*Toldot* 1881, Rabbi Dr. Erin Leib Smokler translation, Noticing the *Nekudah*, November 3, 2021) points out the distinction between the blessing Isaac gives Jacob, "May God give you of the dew of the heaven and the fat of the earth, abundance of new grain and wine"(Gen 27:28) and the one he gives Esau, "Behold, your dwelling places are from the fat of the land, and from the dew of heaven above" (Gen 27:39.) The *Sefat Emet* describes Jacob's blessing as the blessing of a person who is aware of their human vulnerability and is constantly reaffirming their dependence on God. Esau's blessing is for the person who notices what already is, and feels responsible for that which has already been provided. One might say that Jacob's is a blessing of entitlement, while Esau's blessing must be earned. These blessings don't have to be interpreted as mutually exclusive, nor should we associate only one with real faith.

If we jump ahead to the reunion of Jacob and Esau years later (Gen 33:1-11) we see that both Jacob and Esau feel abundantly blessed, and are eager to reconcile with one another. But Jacob feels anxious as he prepares for their reunion. His nervous system is activated. He may have received his brother's birthright, but we might guess that it did not come with a clear conscience. Once he sees that Esau has also been blessed, and feels blessed, he can relax. He can then offer his gifts from a place of love and connection, rather than one of obligation and separation, and Esau is able to accept them.

Let's sit in the spirit of Isaac and Rebecca, whose twins embodied the fullness of God's blessing. Certainty and uncertainty. Desire and satisfaction. Alienation and reconciliation. What is and what is yet to be. Sitting with our eyes closed, breathing in and out, noticing what comes automatically and what needs attention. We let go of that which blocks access to our own faith in God's abiding blessing, in all of its forms and expressions.

Rabbi Nancy Kasten participated in the fourth cohort of the IJS Rabbinic Leadership Program and in Jewish Mindfulness Meditation Teacher Training. She serves as Chief Relationship Officer for Faith Commons, a multifaith organization that lefts up faith voices in the public square for the common good.

Jonathan's humility, honesty, friendship and compassion are the vessels through which his teachings have been implanted in her heart and mind.

Vayeitzei
Coming Home to Our Authentic Selves

Hannah Dresner

The midrash credits Jacob with introducing the *Maariv* prayer. Darkness forces Jacob to pause. Within the private veil of night, he lets down his defenses, turns inward, and takes stock. Perhaps he truly finds himself in a wilderness, cut off from his source and broken open in pain for having sunk to tricking his brother out of birthright and blessing. *Moshe Chayim Ephrayim* writes that it is, indeed, from this humble place of self-knowledge that Jacob reaches out and touches God.

If Shacharit addresses the surprise of our daily rebirth and *Mincha* is a mid-afternoon check-in,

Maariv is our homecoming. Returned from our interactions of the day, back to Self. We return to our deeper, private selves under the cloak of darkness. Reaching out to touch Spirit at the end of the day, letting go of the armor and masks of the day, it is also possible to touch the makom of our authenticity, the place where we truly are, and rest in that truth, whatever it is.

"*Vayifga bamakom, vayalen sham, ki va hashemesh.*" The simple meaning is that Jacob "came to (touched down at) the place, and spent the night there, for the sun had set." But the midrash translates literally: "*vayifga*" means "he touched;" he touched the "*Makom*," "The Presence," the Ever-present Presence, encountering his God as he settled for the night.

Reaching out for God, having let go of the armor of the day, it is also possible to touch the *makom* of our authenticity, the place we truly *are,* and rest in that truth, whatever it is.

"Jacob left *Beer Sheva* and went toward *Haran.*" "...And he reached a certain place... and took one of the stones from this place and used it as his pillow and lay down ...to sleep." "He dreamed, and behold: a ladder stuck in the ground, its top reaching toward heaven, and angels of God ascending and descending upon it."

Moshe Chayyim Ephrayim of Sudilkov teaches that Jacob's dream envisions states of spiritual awareness, and their flux. Sometimes we are in states of *quatnut*, of small mindedness, and at other times we're in states of *gadlut*, of greatness. We move up and down a continuum of consciousness, always either ascending or descending, but never fixed on a particular rung.

Ready to rest, "he took one of the stones from the place to use as his pillow." From where does he take the stone? He takes it from the *makom* - the place - where he un-pretentiously finds himself to be. Coming to rest at *maariv*, when boundaries are soft and introspection is easier, Jacob acknowledges the relative rung of his holiness, and fashions a cushion out of that hard rock of a place upon which to sleep and dream.

May this teaching on *Parashat Vayeitzei* remind us of what an evening practice can be: a reconnection with the core of authenticity we may have fallen away from, negotiating the day's challenges. The invitation is to sit quietly with the events of the day, honest in reviewing the rungs we have traversed; honest in where the experience of the day has left us. And from this *makom*, the *place* in which we find ourselves at evening-time, reach out to *Hamakom*, the Ever-present One, allowing reconnection with the source of divinity always residing within.

Rabbi Hannah Dresner is a long-time friend of all the Slater siblings, and serves as spiritual leader of the oldest Jewish Renewal congregation, Or Shalom in Vancouver BC.

What she loves about Jonathan is his embodiment and teaching of a seamlessly melded mind, spirit and body in Jewish life and practice.

Vayishlach
Panim L'Panim
Seeing the face of God in each other

Karen Glazer Perolman

This collection of Torah insights will be published as we enter the third year of the COVID-19 global pandemic. While wearing face masks undoubtedly protected us from the virus, we became accustomed to not seeing each other *panim-el-panim*, face-to-face.

Parashat Vayishlach tells two stories of seeing each other's faces. First, Jacob wrestles with a Divine figure who injures and blesses him with a new name, Israel. "Jacob named the place *Peniel*, meaning, 'I have seen a divine being face to face, yet my life has been preserved.'" (Genesis 32:31) Then, in the dramatic conclusion to the Jacob and Esau narrative, the brothers reunite after 20 years of estrangement. When offered gifts of livestock and servants Esau refuses, but Jacob presses him: "No, I pray you; if you would do me this favor, accept from me this gift; for to see your face is like seeing the face of God." (Genesis 33:10)

There is a story of the Baal Shem Tov, the founder of Hasidism, who was asked by his students, "Master, how should one determine the hour in which night ends and day begins?" One student suggested, "Is it when a person can distinguish a sheep from a dog in the distance?" "No," said the rabbi, "It is not." A second student ventured, "Is it when one can distinguish a date tree and a fig tree from afar?" "It is not that either," replied the teacher. "Please tell us the answer," the students begged, "How should one determine when night has ended and day begins?" "It is when you look into the face of a stranger and see your sister or brother," said the rabbi. "Until then, night is still with us."

In this story the Besht blends the halakhic with the spiritual–we must know what time the day begins so we know what time to pray. But there is a deeper meaning: the ability to see another's face and distinguish it from that of a stranger is the moment in which a new day begins. When Jacob sees his brother's face, he is able to see more than simply his kid brother whose birthright and blessing he stole, he is able to see Esau's humanity and divinity.

More than ever our world needs each of us to see each other as made in the image of our Creator. In our personal spiritual practice, we have the opportunity to greet ourselves as Jacob and Esau greeted each other—with open arms and generous hearts. The Hebrew word for face is *panim*, a plural noun. Perhaps this is because when we see each other's faces we also have the opportunity to see the face of our Creator.

Rabbi Karen Glazer Perolman is the Senior Associate Rabbi at Congregation B'nai Jeshurun in Short Hills, NJ and was a participant in the third cohort of the IJS Clergy Leadership Program.

Jonathan's wisdom, kindness and vulnerability, will be an enduring dugma (model) for us all.

Vayeshev
Mindfulness in the Physical World

Ben Herman

Parashat Vayeshev begins as follows: "Jacob settled in the land where his father dwelt, the land of Canaan." Aren't the words "where his father dwelt" extraneous?

Rabbi Levi Yitzhak of Berdichev in his work Kedushat Levi explains that the word "dwelt" connotes fear that Jacob did not worship God properly. The phrase "his father" demonstrates that Jacob did have the same fear for God as his father Isaac.

Levi Yitzhak's next point really interests me. He states the following principle: a person needs to understand that all his actions are for the sake of heaven, even those which are physical. When one eats and drinks one must have the intention that this is for the health of his/her body to serve God. When one has sex, the intention must be for the mitzvah of satisfying one's spouse. Acting in this matter will lift the holy sparks found in this physical world.

How often do we engage in the same habits mindlessly, without a second thought? The purpose of Judaism having blessings for everything is to indicate gratitude-that one will pause, be mindful of the experience and be thankful for being in that exact moment. Mindfulness for Levi Yitzhak is not an act that takes place only in the synagogue, rather it must be embedded in every action that one undertakes in life. This is a daunting if not impossible task with so much of life being done on autopilot. By bringing mindful intention to any activity, one recognizes the higher purpose behind the act and develops a greater sense of appreciation for both life and for the Holy One.

Life is full of distractions vying for our attention. Rather than get caught up with those distractions, our job according to Levi Yitzhak is to give our full attention to whatever we are engaged with at the moment. Jacob's settling in the land of Canaan demonstrates that in this physical act he was fully engaged with his relationship with God, just as his father Isaac was. Similarly, we need to be fully present in the physical activities that occur moment by moment in our lives.

A practice: Find a comfortable seated position. Close your eyes. Pay attention to any sounds that you hear, be they birds chirping or a lawnmower. Note any thoughts, feelings or sensations you have and view them as passersby, here one second and gone the next.

After 3-5 minutes of listening to the sounds around you, repeat the mantra הכל בידי שמים, all is in God's hands. Repeat this mantra for 3-5 minutes until you lose focus of everything around you. After repeating the mantra, return to focusing on the sounds around you. See everything as ultimately being in God's hands.

After 2-3 minutes, slowly open your eyes and note the room/environment in which you are in. See if you have increased appreciation for every sound that you have heard.

Rabbi Ben Herman is the spiritual leader of Mosaic Law Congregation, Sacramento, CA.

He appreciates Jonathan's thoughtfulness, especially when he pauses before answering a question. Also, how he says "yes....and."

Miketz
Waking Up to Daily Miracles

Andrea Goldstein

Gen. 41:1 - **After two years' time,** *Pharaoh dreamed that he was standing by the Nile.*

Commenting on this verse, Rabbi Menahem Nahum of Chernobyl writes:

"After two years' time (*sh'natayim yammim*)." *Sh'natayim* signifies sleep (*sheinah*). When the days of sleep end and when we arouse ourselves from the sleep of time and learn with expanded awareness and consciousness, **"Pharaoh dreamed** (*uphar'oh cholem*)": there was a powerful revelation. The appearance of miracles was strengthened.

When the days of sleep end – When we experience a waking up to the fullness of our lives. When we feel the fullness of our lives including all joys and blessings, as well as all sorrow and pains.

And when we arouse ourselves – When we wake ourselves up by engaging in mindfulness practices like silence, meditation, tikkun *middot*, and mindful study and movement.

From the sleep of time – From the constraints of the calendar and clock. When we feel bound by time, deadlines, to-do lists and more often our goal is to simply make it through. The deadlines or the tasks themselves are not at issue. Instead, we must ask ourselves how we relate to those time bound commitments. Are we so focused on checking something off the list that we miss the actual experience of what we are doing? Or so focused on getting out the door in the morning that we forget to taste the coffee or eggs that we made for breakfast?

Learn with expanded awareness and consciousness – In this awakened state we are more open to learning from every experience, no matter how small. Each breath expands our awareness, and we are able to connect to a greater consciousness by being fully present, moment to moment, breath by breath, without judgment or fear.

Pharaoh dreamed – Do not think this means that sleep has overtaken our lives once more. Instead, as Rabbi Nahum notes, *cholem* is connected to *chalim*, meaning to become healthy or whole. When we are spiritually awake, we experience a sense of wellbeing and rootedness that allows us to connect with the oneness of all life, regardless of how broken the world can sometimes feel.

The appearance of miracles was strengthened – From the place of spiritual attunement we notice miracles everywhere.

Rabbi Andrea Goldstein has served as a rabbi at Congregation Shaare Emeth in St. Louis, Missouri for 24 years and is the founder and director of the Jewish Mindfulness Center of St. Louis.

She loves that Jonathan teaches the study of Torah as a spiritual practice, and the way his whole face lights up when he shares a teaching that brings him such obvious delight.

Vayigash
Entering Emptiness

Tirzah Firestone

"וְלֹא יָכֹל יוֹסֵף לְהִתְאַפֵּק...וַיִּקְרָא הוֹצִיאוּ כל אִישׁ מֵעָלָי"

"And Joseph could no longer restrain himself...and he called out: Remove every person from my presence!" Then he reveals himself to his brothers saying: "*I am Joseph your brother, whom you sold to Egypt.*"

Joseph has created a trap for his brothers in what seems like a tormenting game of cat and mouse. Is he on a power trip? Or is this vengeance for all that his brothers had put him through years earlier? And why does Joseph reveal himself with the words: "*your brother whom you sold to Egypt?*" Couldn't he have simply said: I am your brother Joseph." The rest they already knew.

Rabbi Shalom Noah Berezovsky (the Slonimer Rebbe, 1911-2000) likens this moment of denouement to the יְחוּד עֶלְיוֹן of the High Priest in the Holy of Holies on Yom Kippur when he rose to the level of angels, leaving behind all personal attachment and identity. Similarly, Joseph and his brothers "removed all persons," meaning, they removed their personal identities from the scene. Therefore, Torah says "*no person stood with him*" when Joseph revealed himself.

Joseph knew prophetically that his brothers needed to prepare for the long descent into exile by strengthening themselves with holiness. He knew that only one who has absented themselves from their יֵשׁוּת, their substance or ego, can commune with the strengthening power of divinity. For when we are ensconced in our personal identities, we cannot enter this holy place. Therefore, he tormented his brothers until they got to the point where they were in a state of אַיִן וְאֶפֶס, nothingness.

This is why Joseph adds the words "(I am your brother) whom you sold into Egypt." As the *B'er Mayim Chayyim* (R' Chaim of Chernowitz) says: I am Yosef, the one and the same that you sold. Lest you think that in my own eyes I have become great, know that I am the same Yosef whom you sold as a slave. I was broken then and I am still broken (and egoless) now.

The Torah is teaching us that to commune with Hashem, we need first to "remove all persons," that is, put aside our ego's attachments and identifications and with deepest humility, enter a state of emptiness, אַיִן וְאֶפֶס. There we can commune with the Holy One and gather the strength we need for the trials ahead.

Rabbi Dr. Tirzah Firestone is an author, Jungian therapist, and Rabbi Emerita of Congregation Nevei Kodesh in Boulder, Colorado,

She appreciates Jonathan's tireless devotion to imparting Hasidic wisdom, which has has inspired an entire generation.

Vayechi
"Assemble and Listen:"
Practicing *Dibbuk Chaverim*

Andy Vogel

As the Book of Genesis closes, our patriarch Jacob models for his children what makes sacred community holy. As his life begins to wane, Jacob summons all his children to his bedside, and commands them:

> "Assemble [*he'kabtzu*] and listen [*v'shim'u*], O children of Jacob / Listen [*v'shim'u*] to [*el*] Israel your father" (Genesis 49:2).

The verse is strange, notes the *Ma'or Va'Shemesh* (Kalonymous Kalman Epstein, Krakow, 1753-1825). Isn't the two-fold repetition of the verb "listen" redundant in the verse? And wouldn't Jacob understand that the purpose of their gathering is not that they listen to him, but rather that they be more attentive to God's word?

The Ma'or Va'Shemesh clarifies: Yes, when ten Jews gather to form a *minyan*, the Divine Presence comes to rest upon them (Sanhedrin 39a); and Divine blessings come to them if they perceive God's Presence and, in humility, if each person makes themselves smaller to make space for God, to make space for the other. When Jacob requests that they "listen" and "listen" again, the Ma'or Va'Shemesh teaches, he is instructing them to engage in a careful kind of dialogue, that each one truly listen to the other.

This is the practice of *Dibbuk Chaverim*, "cleaving to one's friends," when we gather in a holy community of trusted friends, family and students. The Ma'or Va'Shemesh teaches that the key aspect to this kind of sacred intentional meeting, *kibbutz* ("assembly"), involves "gathering oneself toward one's friend," and nullifying one's ego in the act of careful listening, to hear and understand from our friend how they serve God.

He goes on to teach through a brilliant switch of Hebrew vowels in the verse that Jacob was playfully reminding them that the power of careful listening brings down the Divine Presence. The *Ma'Or Va'Shemesh* re-translates the verse, by playing with the vowel in the word *el* ("to") and switching out the three-dot *seigol* for the two-dot *tzeireh* – transforming the little preposition into *El* (God). The end of the verse now reads, "Listen to the God of Israel, who is your [Divine] Father." By listening to one another's Torah, and then to Jacob's own words of Torah, the children will in fact be listening to the Divine Presence dwelling among them, blessing them with expanded consciousness, love and compassion.

Practice:

How can you engage in *Dibbuk Chaverim*, close listening to your friends?

In listening, when do you choose to "nullify" your ego, and in what ways?

Pay close attention when they speak to the ways that they choose to serve the Divine, to pursue their Truths. What can you learn from them?

Rabbi Andrew Vogel is the senior rabbi at Temple Sinai in Brookline, MA.

He had the pleasure of learning with Rabbi Jonathan Slater in the first cohort of the IJS Clergy Leadership ProgramIJS's CLP-1 (2014-15), and was deeply moved by Jonathan's passion for Hasidut, yoga and poetry that touches on the dilemmas of being human, and for his humility and rich sense of humor.

Va-eira
Drawing on Truth
Remembering Who We Are

Joey Wolf

Degel Machaneh Ephraim: *"Moreover I heard the cry of the children of Israel, in that Mitzrayim worked them, and I remembered my covenant. . ." (Exodus 6:5)*

Why does the Ba'al Shem Tov react to the verse "Egypt would know that I am God," (Ex. 7:5). He suggests that it's strange that God would go to the effort to produce signs and wonders, to ransack the cupboard up in the Divine Kitchen (as it were), to flip nature's order, just so that Egypt would come intimately into the Divine Presence?

Instead, the truth is that this "Mitzrayim-ness" applies to us Jews, for we are the ones who *enact Mitzrayim* – and are sunk in falsehood. Our service to God (so frequently) arises from what's artificial. Extraordinarily, the Holy One down streamed the light of the *Shekhinah*, so that we would realize that nothing operates in the world save for Divine Power. If we perceive even (the tiniest) glimmer of Truth, we can rise to the greatest heights and our heart-faith expands. . .

The Israelites cry out to extricate themselves from despair and they long for Truth. *"And I remembered my covenant. . ."* As one awakens the mind, so there's an awakening from above. Since this awakening comes via Truth (*tiferet*), there is a thruway that conveys us from purposelessness to the Infinite, the beginning of everything until the furthest point away as it says "I am first and I am last/*ani rishon ve-ani acharon*" (Isaiah 44:6).

Practice:
The Degel suggests that we routinely live our lives closed off, *in Mitzrayim*, from Divine Truth. We are forgetful! And yet – we can open our minds up to who we *are*, or where we get our life's force.

In your meditation, focus first on a moment (a place or another person) going back to when you were very young. Marinate yourself in someone's kindness, a smiling face, a backyard scene, a loving embrace. Afterward, feel the *trunk* of your life, your essence, what you are proudest of having become, or exude to others. Lastly, imagine yourself leaving behind an impression, growing physically weaker, but having taught or left something that's lasting and good. Endings and beginnings. Spend 5-10 minutes on each piece. Bring whole-iness into your day - be seen (as in *Va-eira*) truthfully. It's pretty wonderful to think of all the signs and wonders being performed – just for you!

Rabbi Joey Wolf is the rabbi emeritus at Havurah Shalom, Portland, Oregon.

Jon and he entered JTS together in 1974 on a bleary morning. Together, they formed a chavruta for Talmud study, penetrated the obscure mysteries of the text (thanks to his guidance); and unlocked the doldrums of the Seminary. Jonathan's quiet humility and quirky humor, the sparkle in his eye, are forever with him

Bo
When You Encounter the Dark Side

Toba August

The Zohar asks why this parashah uses the word *"Bo"* or "come" to Pharoah instead of *"Lekh"* – "go" to Pharoah, (Zohar, Vol. II 34b translated: Daniel Matt). It says that Moses had to "enter into" his darkest fears. Perhaps feeling unworthy, Moses was afraid to face the evil side of Pharoah. The Zohar describes how God brought Moses into chamber after chamber, to a high rung where he encountered the "Mystery of the great serpent". The "mystery" was the truth that a primordial dark side exists simultaneously with goodness and light. Only with the help of God was Moses able to face this fear and encounter Pharaoh equally with power and authority.

Like Moses, for us to become our best selves, we need a "come to Pharoah moment." Facing our fears means that we acknowledge our "shadow self," a painful acceptance of our limitations, and disappointments.

When we practice mindfulness, we can face our dark side.

Take a few moments to sit and be present with your breath.

See if you can imagine what Moses felt when he was told to "come to" Pharoah.

Have you ever felt this way?

Keep breathing, and be curious about your fears and lack of confidence during a challenging encounter.

Can you name that fear? What does it look and feel like? Does this fear affect your current behavior?

Say to yourself, *"Bo L' Pharaoh."* "It's time to come to Pharoah"

I can embrace this difficult place and forgive myself.

I can do *teshuvah* and return to wholeness.

I can have compassion for my 'shadow' and accept this aspect of myself.

I can continue to live fully with courage and joy.

When you are ready, open your eyes, and read this poem:

Go to the Limits of Your Longing
Rainer Maria Rilke

God speaks to each of us as he makes us,
then walks with us silently out of the night.
These are the words we dimly hear:
You, sent out beyond your recall,
go to the limits of your longing.
Embody me.
Flare up like a flame
and make big shadows I can move in.
Let everything happen to you: beauty and terror.
Just keep going. No feeling is final.
Don't let yourself lose me.
Nearby is the country they call life.
You will know it by its seriousness.
Give me your hand.
Now, take a few more deep breaths, and know you can regularly
encounter your shadow side with kindness and not be afraid.

*Rabbi Toba August enjoys teaching, studying and attending IJS Hevra-
ya retreats. For her, Jonathan has been an inspiring teacher, caring mentor
and friend.*

Beshallach
Singing a Change of Heart

Joanna Selznick Dulkin

Singing can be transformative and healing: it changes both our lived experience and our experience of the Divine. In *Beshallach*, the act of singing brings about a change of heart: the broken hearts of the newly freed Israelites are the same broken-open hearts that make for expansive healing, joyful song and dance at the shores of the sea. Moses and Miriam's invitation to communal song leads the Israelites to a new relationship with God, from *Adonai – ish- milchamah* (Warrior-God, Ex. 15:3) to *Adonai rofe-kha* (God your Healer, Ex. 15:26).

Rabbi Nachman of Bratzlav teaches us that song, and the voices that sing it, can bring about peace and wholeness. Using the incipit to Miriam's song as his prooftext, Rabbi Nachman teaches that "through the concept of the voice, one merits peace." He reveals this peace encoded in Miriam's invitation to sing: *Va ta'an lahem Miriam, shiru l'Adonai* וַתַּעַן לָהֶם מִרְיָם שִׁירוּ. When re-arranged, the first letter of each word reveals the word שלום. (Likutei Moharan 27:8). When we give voice to our prayers as Miriam did, with a call and a response, singing itself becomes an act of renewal. Like our ancestors at the sea, our voices can transport us from fear to possibility. Each of our unique voices can be an instrument for wholeness, renewal - for peace.

Inviting in one's voice can be intimidating, especially for people who have been told that they "can't sing." Just for today (and maybe one day for forever), tell that voice that whispers "You can't sing!" to take a hike.

Breathe into this quiet space acceptance, love, or curiosity for your unique singing voice. It is here that you might be able to hear the invitation from Miriam to join her: *VaTa'an Li Miriam Shiru L'Adonai!*

Close your eyes, and begin to slow your breathing, in and out through the nose.

Let the tongue rest at the bottom of the mouth. Relax the cheeks, the space between your eyebrows, the shoulders. Unclench the teeth.

See how lightly you can touch the lips together.

Can you make even more space inside your closed mouth, soft palate and throat?

Take another deep breath through the nose, and exhale in a hum. Keep the hum going with each exhale, for 3-5 breaths. As you hum, feel the resonance of your voice radiating against your lips, tickling the inside of the nasal cavities, filling the throat. This is the root of your voice.

When you are ready, give your hum a shape: the word Shalom.

Use the length of the entire breath to sing three "Shaloms" into being, using one to two tones that feel effortless and easy. Know that with each Shalom, you are giving voice to wholeness.

After three Shaloms, take a few regular breaths, and allow yourself to feel the effects of this practice.

Hazzan Joanna Dulkin of Adath Jeshurun in Minnetonka, MN, was lucky to become Jonathan's student early in her career, and was a member of the second cohort of the IJS Cantorial Leadership Program. His wisdom, humor and dugma isheet (personal example) has been invaluable to the continuing growth of her mind and soul.

Parashat Yitro
"God's Call Can Still Be Heard—If We Listen"

Jacob Staub

Moses ascends the mountain to meet God and receive the divine revelation, while the Israelites stand below amidst intense thunder and lightning, each hearing something unique according to their individual capacities.

What did they hear? Is there a way to read Exodus 19 as more than a mythic narration of the giving of the Torah at Mount Sinai—as a way into an understanding about how each of us can encounter God today? The Hasidic Rebbe Arele Roth (1894-1947) thinks so.

Along with his rabbinic predecessors, Reb Arele believes that the Voice that Moses heard at Sinai never ceased to sound and continues to call today. In fact, he understands this sub-audible voice to be the reason that people do *teshuvah* (repentance). That is, the vibrations of the Voice—the same Voice as the one that Moses heard at Sinai—move us imperceptibly to yearn for that which is beyond hearing, beyond seeing, beyond understanding. The Voice calls perpetually in a whisper: *Return, My wayward children.* Most of us are unable hear this call most of the time because of all the noise and day-to-day distractions in our lives. It requires silence and focus to hear the Voice, to sense the divine Presence.

In other words, according to Reb Arele, divine revelation has never ceased! It continues to this very moment and is potentially accessible to everyone. If we unclutter our minds and practice listening to the divine, we can hear it.

There are many ways to quiet our mind and listen in a different way. A meditation or chanting practice is one alternative. We bring attention to our breath or to the sounds of the chant. We learn to remain in this moment, letting go of memories or future planning. In this moment, we attend to our deepest yearning. Beyond our concerns about our ambition, our work, our family, our finances, we listen to the innermost yearnings of our heart. What is most precious? What are the connections we most long for? We notice what arises, and if we are fortunate, what we perceive is the divine call from Sinai beckoning us to return.

Rabbi Jacob Staub is Professor Emeritus of Jewish Philosophy and Spirituality at the Reconstructionist Rabbinical College.

He and his weekly hevruta partner, Rabbi Amy Eilberg, have studied the Hasidic texts that Jonathan has selected and have been inspired and transformed by that study.

Mishpatim
The Structures That Support Us, Support God

Megan Doherty

In his writing on *Mishpatim*, the *Netivot Shalom* brings forward the rabbinic idea that the creation of the universe emerges from God's desire for a *dira batachtonim* - a dwelling place (in modern Hebrew, an apartment) in *this* world - *olam hazeh*. God desires companionship, relationship, and a dynamic experience. God, for the Netivot Shalom, doesn't want to create a perfect system of a universe that will run beautifully by itself and can be admired from a distance; God wants a world to play with and dance with and love and live within.

But there is a problem. God and God's word are pure *emet*, truth. This world, the world of humans with all of our fallibility and frailty, is full of illusions, delusions, dreams, and outright lies. The naked transparency of Divine clarity and justice can't co-exist with the blurriness and ambiguity of the world-as-it-is.

Yetziat Mitzrayim, the exodus from Egypt, is the beginning of God's solution: the people Israel choose God so that God can 'dwell among them/us.' On Mt. Sinai, with the giving of the Ten Words, God shows us the outline for what God's dwelling place will look like. Perhaps surprisingly, it doesn't look like a physical space. It is a set of instructions for how we relate to God and to each other. God's dwelling place is us. At that point, it's all still a bit abstract and high level. What is Shabbat practice actually supposed to be like? What does it mean to honor one's parents? Where is the line between 'admiring' and coveting'?

We come to *Mishpatim*. The first set of instructions in the Torah for how we messy and complicated humans can live in community, comity, and justice with each other. These instructions fill in some of the details of the overview we got at Sinai. By following them, we begin to fulfill God's desire to dwell within and among us. In our world of illusions, *Mishpatim* tells us that we make space for the Divine when we see the divine spark in each human, treat each other fairly, and build systems which care for the most vulnerable among us.

Practice:
As you walk in the world, notice the systems that sustain you and your communities, and the individual souls that sustain the systems. In each moment, notice the opportunity you have to make all the concentric circles of connection in your life a beautiful dwelling place for God.

Rabbi Megan Doherty is a proud alum of both the Rabbinic Leadership and Jewish Mindfulness Meditation Teacher Training Programs of IJS. Learning hasidic texts with Jonathan during her cohort and in the years afterward profoundly transformed her relationship to both Hasidut and text study and for that, there are not enough words to express her gratitude and love.

Terumah
The Mishkan Within

Kimberly Herzog Cohen

It was a cold Sunday morning, but when I walked into the Temple classroom, I placed my hand on my heart and felt a sense of comforting warmth. The *2nd* graders were standing in a circle, throwing a ball of yarn, creating a magnificent web. Immediately, I was brought back to the closing ritual as our IJS Clergy Leadership Program cohort spun a visual reminder of our interconnectedness.

Parashat Terumah includes the word: וְעָשׂוּ לִי מִקְדָּשׁ וְשָׁכַנְתִּי בְּתוֹכָם (Ex 25:8) – And let them make Me a sanctuary that I may dwell among them.

Parashat Terumah emphasizes the work of cultivating our souls so that we can engage with the world more thoughtfully and more powerfully. There are so many pathways and possibilities through which we can tune into a deeper consciousness. This involves the work of sitting in silence, of raising our voices in song, of study, of movement, and of building relationships across race and class.

This deeper consciousness and connection can become obscured because the world barrages us with painful realities, either imagined or real, that cause us great stress and evoke feelings of deep angst. The sacred words of *Parashat Terumah* reminds us: we must build again and again a *Mishkan* in our hearts and among each other to hold pain and joy and then stand with a resolute sense of responsibility. As noted by the *Or HaChaim*, a true light in the 18*th* century Moroccan Jewish community and in the hasidic movement, the Torah text "does not say 'within it,' [ie, the *Mishkan*] which means that the place that God will sanctify to dwell is within the children of Israel that encircle the Tabernacle..." (R. Eliyahu Munk, Lambda Publishers, 1998)

The *Or HaChaim* did not create a physical representation of our interconnectedness through yarn, however, an eternal spiritual truth stands through time: the Shechinah dwells among us – at Brandeis-Bardin, in a second-grade classroom in Dallas, over Zoom sessions with a chevruta partner, and in all the moments when we can be fully present.

V'asu li mikdash v'shakhanti b'tokham—Make for me a holy place and I will dwell among you. As we continually construct the tabernacle of our souls, may we do so with the conviction that all the places in which we dwell here on earth be places of safety, be places of shared vision and just action, be places where the *Shekhinah* is recognized within all God's creatures.

Rabbi Kimberly Herzog Cohen serves as a spiritual leader at Temple Emanue-El in Dallas TX and is forever grateful for R. Jonathan Slater's warm sense of humor and energetic Torah discussions.

Tetzaveh
A Light in the Dark

Cantor Sharon Kohn and Cantor Louise Treitman

...l'ha-alot ner — tamid.
As for you, you shall command the Israelites,
that they take you clear oil of beaten olives for the light;
to kindle a lamp — perpetually.
Exodus 27:20

This portion, *Tetzaveh*, details the priestly work that will be done in the *Mishkan*, the tabernacle. The first task is to create light. The priest is instructed "to kindle a lamp *tamid*." How do we understand this phrase and, more specifically, the word *tamid*? Rashi says if we pay close attention to the *te'amim* (cantillation/ trope marks), a clear meaning will emerge. What does he mean? The cantillation marks in the Torah serve as an intricate punctuation system, indicating which words go together. In the phrase "to kindle a lamp *tamid*," the trope signals that the words *l'ha-alot* (to light) and *ner* (a lamp) are connected to each other. The word *tamid* is separated from the preceding words. Therefore, *tamid* modifies the verb and should be translated as "regularly / continually / perpetually." On this specific portion, Rashi says "Doing something every single night may be termed 'continually/*tamid*.'"

The Sefat Emet applies this understanding of *tamid* to spiritual practice. He shares two deeper meanings: "... a person should do every mitzvah with the intention that some of its illumination will truly remain eternal." Something of the light shines on beyond the time of the lighting. Something remains even after we have finished our spiritual practice of meditating, praying or yoga. The second meaning of the lighting is in the timing - the priest did the lighting at night. The Sefat Emet says that this practice "was a form of preparation: the light of the *menorah* of the *Mishkan* [helped prepare us] for the days of exile, which are called 'nights.'"

We can no longer kindle the light in the *Mishkan*. We **can** do something *tamid,* such as the nighttime *Sh'ma,* a weekly yoga class or a daily meditation. In addition to the value we get out of the activity itself, like the light, the benefit will remain long after.

Practice: Take a few moments each day to sit - make this a *tamid* commitment. Feel the light - the *ner* - within you: the light of Torah, the light of God, the light of love. As your breathing slows, allow the light to shine throughout your body. Keep returning to the light. Continue to sit with this light for your chosen time. Know that the light will remain long after you open your eyes. Know that the light will help you through the dark times.

Cantor Louise Treitman and Cantor Sharon Kohn are IJS hevruta partners who have been meeting "tamid" (regularly) for many years.

Cantor Treitman is Cantor Emerita of Temple Beth David in Westwood, Massachusetts and serves on the faculty of Hebrew College. She studied with Jonathan in the first Clergy Leadership Program and loves his gracious and creative way of weaving Hasidic texts together with mindfulness and meditation.

Cantor Sharon Kohn works as an Interim Cantor and was introduced to Hasidic thought by Jonathan in the first Clergy Leadership Program. His commitment to the material, to being present to and for his students has opened new ways of being for her.

Ki Tisa
Here the Rocks Came to be Forgiven

Sheila Peltz Weinberg

We meet our whole selves in this Torah portion. We are the ones building the *Mishkan*, the desert sanctuary. It will connect us to the source of our liberation and guide us in this wilderness. We are the ones preparing the special oils and incense that evoke the sacred. We are the ones using our skill to construct an altar, a vessel of communication to the highest. We are the ones who make the deep commitment to keep the Sabbath. Yes, and we are the ones who are impatient when our leader, Moses, is so long in coming down from the mountain. Yes, we are the ones who beseech Aaron to make a golden calf. We gleefully toss in our precious jewelry, dancing and singing in praise of our idol, our delusion.

We meet ourselves in Moses as well. And in God. We meet ourselves in the feeling of being betrayed at this propitious moment. We meet ourselves as Moses begs God to remain in relationship with Israel, God's people. We meet Moses when he hurls the tablets, inscribed with God's finger. They shatter. We are witnesses or perpetrators of violence. We see our people consumed and perish in the plague. We taste the consequences of our betrayal and our ignorance. It is bitter.

This, of course, is not the end. There is no end. The story continues. There is journey, not arrival.

Moses inscribes a second set of tablets. He is invited to hide in the cleft of the Rock. Moses will see God's back and hear the words of God's love and forgiveness. Moses receives this. In later years, the rabbis will edit these 13 phrases, so they embody pure love, patience, and forgiveness. A sleight of hand perhaps or exactly what we need to keep going.

The great Hasidic master Nahman of Bratzlav said: "If you believe it is possible to break, believe that it is possible to repair." Another Hasidic master, Menahem Mendel of Kotzk added, "There is nothing so whole as a broken heart." These wise men could have been commenting on this Torah portion of brokenness, profound confusion, longing and healing.

The neo-Hasidic Israeli poet Rivka Miriam takes the text to new depths of wisdom:

Here the rocks came to be forgiven
Because they couldn't move
And the heights came to receive compassion
For being so distant from earth.
The sea swallowed its waves, embarrassed for being restless.
Only forgiveness itself, weak-finned
Pure as lightening that doesn't burn.
Didn't know from whom to beg forgiveness.
Only forgiveness itself
Blurred as the line between dusk and sunset
Fell on its knees before itself.

You are invited to fall on your knees before yourself.

Allow yourself to be held by the deepest compassion and care you have ever known.

Just breathe. In and out.

Let the balm of patience, kindness and love pour over you. Any image or memory will do. A felt sense.

Just breathe.

Let any hurt and anger, fear or confusion, judgment and doubt soften.
Let it all be included in the great love.

The Eternal and Everlasting
Can hold it all.

Rabbi Sheila Peltz Weinberg is a spiritual director and writer, and one of the founders of the Institute for Jewish Spirituality.

Jonathan Slater is her dear friend, teacher and colleague; someone to laugh with, learn with and always feel deeply heard.

Pekudei
Simplicity and Hearing the Voice of God

Gordon Tucker

Shemot (Exodus), alone among the Five Books, finishes in an un-equivocally upbeat way, with the triumph of the completion of the *Mishkan*, and the overwhelming joy of sensing God's Presence in the work of the Israelites' hands. I've always loved the end of *Pekudei* for that reason, but that love is tempered by a sober recognition of what the creation of even the most beautiful institutions of religion can threaten to bring with it.

The cautionary message is contained in a commentary by Mordecai Yosef Leiner of Izbica, in the work *Mei Ha-Shiloach*. The preacher notes that there are eight reports of Moses carrying out the instructions for setting up the appurtenances of the *Mishkan*. In the first seven of them, it is said that when Moses did so, it was "just as God had commanded Moses". But in the eighth, and final act — the setting up of the outermost enclosure of the Tabernacle — that mantra of a phrase suddenly disappears, and it simply says that Moses completed the tasks.

Mordecai Yosef explains: We are meant to take "just as God had commanded Moses" to mean that Moses heard the very same Voice that he had heard at Sinai now commanding him in real time as each task was completed. And as long as the Tabernacle was not completed, Moses was able to hear that Voice, because it was not confined, but was instead ubiquitous throughout the wilderness. However, in driving in the last stake anchoring the courtyard hangings, Moses was necessarily outside the now-completed *Mishkan*. And God's voice was now confined to the interior of the new edifice. Moses could no longer hear it. Thus, "just as God had commanded Moses" no longer applied. It was memory, not Presence.

The idea that God's commanding voice is "locked up" in the elaborately constructed, and highly restricted, institution of worship is so different from the original command (Exodus 20:21) to make "an altar of earth" in any and every place. It warns us that as necessary as institutions may be for providing a locus for our religious needs, we should never lose sight of the fact that they always have the potential of distancing us, rather than drawing us close. As the Kedushat Levi trenchantly notes (commentary on Deuteronomy 27:10), there is a profound religious difference between heeding the words of Torah and heeding the voice of God.

Practice:
The Shakers famously sang of "simple gifts". Consider the ways in which simplicity, and thus greater immediacy (a modern equivalent of an altar of earth) can be re-introduced into our religious practices. Perhaps it can begin ritually with truly eating with simplicity on Pesach, and dwelling in simplicity on Sukkot. And ethically, in promoting responsible uses of technology, so that everywhere on God's earth can be a place where the glorious Voice of creation can be heard by all.

Rabbi Gordon Tucker is the Vice Chancellor for Religious Life and Engagement at Jewish Theological Seminary, a Senior Fellow at the Shalom Hartman Institute of North America, and Senior Rabbi Emeritus at Temple Israel Center of White Plains, NY.

Meeting and learning from the prolific and compassionate scholarship of Rabbi Jonathan Slater (whose teaching also introduced me to the spiritual depths in Mei Shiloach) was the gift given to him by the Institute for Jewish Spirituality in the third cohort of its Rabbinic Leadership Program.

Vayikra
When is a Mitzvah not a Mitzvah?

Jeffrey Goldwasser

When is a mitzvah not a mitzvah? When is it actually a sin?

In *Parashat Vayikra*, we find this verse, "When a person sins unwittingly from any of Adonai's mitzvot, a thing not to be done, and does one of them…" (Leviticus 4:2). The simple interpretation of the verse would be to say that it refers to sins – doing something that God has forbidden. Levi Yitzhak of Berdichev thought it would be more interesting to think about it differently. What if the phrase "sins…from Adonai's mitzvot" means, "sins committed by doing one of the mitzvot?"

This early master of Hasidism observed that: "When you commit a transgression and you know it, you feel your heart break inside you and you return to God in repentance. However, when you do a mitzvah and you glorify yourself in it, you think highly of yourself and fill yourself with pride over it. You say to yourself, 'I have added to the riches of the Holy Blessed One!'"

That, says Levi Yitzhak, is a much more dangerous place to be than just committing a sin. A person who turns the performance of a mitzvah into an opportunity to get a swelled head of self-righteous glory is much less likely to even recognize that such behavior is truly sinful. Levi Yitzhak boldly states that such behavior is "no mitzvah at all." He says: "Rather, it is a transgression. It is called a sin."

Does that mean that a person should not feel good about writing a check to help the needy? Does it cancel out the good you have done if you take pleasure in studying Torah? Of course not. The mitzvot are intended to bring joy into our lives, but it is the joy of joining ourselves to God, not of inflating our opinion of ourselves.

Here is a practice you can try. The next time you do something wonderful – anything from making a donation to a worthy cause to lighting Shabbat candles – take a moment to close your eyes, take in a deep breath, and ask yourself, "For whom am I doing this?" When you identify the ego within your mitzvah – the self-satisfying motivation within you – blow it out of you on your next exhale.

Then, on your next breath in, let the awareness within you grow that your action is a response to the Holy One who has given you life and filled you with blessings. Notice the joy that grows within as you realize that you are giving back to your Source.

Rabbi Jeff Goldwasser is the spiritual leader of Temple Sinai in Cranston, Rhode Island.

He is grateful to Rabbi Jonathan Slater for making beautiful Hasidic teachings like this one from Levi Yitzhak available to multitudes of people and for his deeply insightful commentaries upon them.

Tzav
The Fire is already Burning

Michael Bernstein

"A perpetual fire shall be kept burning on the altar, not to go out" (Lev. 6:6).

The *Be'er Mayyim Chayyim* on Lev. 6:1 teaches that we fulfill upon the altar of our own heart these commandments and sacrifices. The text emphasizes the need that the fire not be ready beside the altar, but already burning with intensity. That fire, which is the passion to love and serve God, must precede the "wood," the Torah as a Tree of Life. Then come the sacrifices: the *olah* that ascends only to the divine and the *shelamim*, the wellbeing/peace offering divided between the sanctified portions and that which is eaten for blessing and enjoyment.

This teaching focuses on the different strata underlying our experiences of material fulfillment. A delicious meal or sense of pleasure is part of the *shelamim*, an offering of wholeness. Knowing that what I perceive as something whole is actually only a part allows me to search for the part that is given through the kohanim to God. What spiritual or emotional labor, what sacrifice goes alongside this enjoyment? When I savor a bite of food, gratitude arises not only from appreciating its pleasant taste and texture but in thinking about the hands that prepared it or picked it or shipped it. The conditions of production cannot be ignored if I am to properly appreciate the bite.

The *olah* transcends my pleasure or awareness of the hidden blessings. The *olah* opens the understanding of the material world as a manifestation of God's existence. It is not only a reminder of the divine but a link to the Divine pleasure in my enjoyment of the world. Each taste and swallow are no longer a material act but a connection to God through the Torah and its laws and lessons. The wood itself is aflame with the hidden Torah as a Tree of Life. Even the rules and spoken blessings that attend my enjoyment of the world have dropped away. There is only a desire to bring joy to my creator who delights in the Torah that remains burning upon the altar of my heart. If I can reach that place, that glimpse of the perpetual fire, then I can once more ignite the wood to burn the offering. I can be ready for the wellbeing/peace sacrifice, some of which serves a heavenly purpose and some finds its way to me to be appreciated and enjoyed.

Rabbi Michael Bernstein is the spiritual leader of Congregation Gesher L'Torah in Alpharetta Georgia.
He found himself called to a new dimension of appreciation for the world around him through seeing sources that he thought he knew through the brilliant lens of Jonathan's Torah.

Shemini
Scuba Diving After Tragedy

Neil F. Blumofe

We stand in the haunting silence after the death of the two boys. This is Aaron's silence; the silence of a grieving father. (Leviticus 10:3) The silence of the abyss. It is the opposite of the still small voice, which invites us to exit from within Elijah's cave, directing us towards discernment and curiosity out in the world. (I Kings 19:13) Here, there is no voice. Nadav and Avihu took up incense, hoping to make a connection to everything. As it teaches in the Zohar: what is *ketoret? It is the ketira of everything.* (Bemidbar 121b) They tried to erase the boundaries between the human creation and the Divine. They hoped to stand in the light of God in the moment, without wearing protective garments. The *Mei HaShiloach* explains*: the boys wanted to bring themselves close to God, looking into the hidden depths, and they wanted to stand on the refined, undressed truth of the conduct of the holy God.* (*Mei HaShiloach*, Volume 1, Shemini)

They were warned. This stepping forward was not commanded. They went too deep without wearing protective gear. They needed a garment to mediate their discoveries before the supernal light. They were to have offered their connection to all, wearing the *me'il* – the coat made entirely of sky-blue wool (*tekhelet*). This represents intense *yirat shamayim*. Without this awe, the power of everything flowed too strongly and faltered their hearts. The *me'il* balances us in our quest to listen. We are not to listen without preparation.

There is valor in taking chances to make connections. Yet we must be prepared and wear the refinements that will bring us back safely. The world is alive in the places we cannot readily see. We must properly affix our regulator, made of *tekhelet*, before our dive – to safely slip into the *me'il* as we journey into the highest realms. We take up our censers, protected, and we follow Rabbi Akiva safely into and out of the realm of paradise. (BT Hagiga 14b).

As we pray for Aaron and ourselves: may the clothes of our mourning become the raiment of our joy. May we distinguish and draw distance from the poignant sundered heart into the resounding, thin pulse of God, in what and how we dare to approach the ineffable.

Practice:

As we close our eyes and gently exhale, what surfaces (again!) behind our eyes that brings us sadness, grief, or shame? Can we meet this heaviness in our solidarity with Aaron? As we notice our mind racing, can we calm our internal tension? Can we exist for a moment in this entombing silence? May our calming breath be our regulator. May our meditative wisdom traditions be our me'il. May we go forward into this silence, noticing the dappled grandeur; the magnificent wreck that has brought us to be who we are in this resounding present moment? It is all beauty. Breathe, again. More deeply we go.

Rabbi Neil F. Blumofe serves as Senior Rabbi of Congregation Agudas Achim in Austin, Texas. He considers Jonathan to be a master and musical guide and teacher who has helped to open Torah of the head, heart, and hand.

Tazria
The Circle Keeps Turning

Debra Robbins

עשרים ושתים אותיות יסוד קבועות בגלגל ברל״א שערים וחוזר
הגלגל פנים
ואחור וזהו סימן לדבר אין בטובה למעלה מענג ואין ברעה
למטה מנגע:

There are twenty-two foundational letters, fixed [by the Holy One] in a circle with two hundred and thirty-one gates. The circle goes forward and back with no beginning or end. There is nothing better than ענג *oneg/joy and nothing worse than* נגע *negah/affliction.*

Over and over, in nearly every paragraph of the Torah portion, the same word.

If a person has a *negah*…

When the *negah* is reported…

Someone examines the *negah*…

Sometimes the *negah* spreads…

Finally, the *negah* comes to an end.

The Torah is not a medical text, it is a sacred guidebook
and so, in Parashat Tazria,
negah is treated as a skin affliction,
public health safety measures are detailed,
rituals for physical cleansing are specified,
and spiritual re-entry into the community is possible.
The verses speak about an ancient medical challenge,
and our own afflictions of:
addiction and boredom,
fear, grief and heartbreak,
loneliness,
regret and sickness,
yearning…
seemingly one for every letter of the alphabet.
The alphabet, all twenty-two Hebrew letters,

God's building blocks of creation,
are also ours.

The Gerer Rebbe taught his community to spin the alphabet wheel of *Sefer Yetzirah*.

Read them one way, and the letters spell, *negah*, (*nun, gimel* and *ayin*)

rotate them around and there is *oneg*, (*ayin, nun, gimel*), the word for joy.

He noticed, and now we do too,
the final letter of the word *negah*, plague, is the Hebrew letter *ayin*,

which is also the Hebrew word for "eye" (the part of the body not the pronoun).

Move the *ayin* from the end to the beginning, and it becomes *oneg* (which doesn't really mean cookies after services).

Oneg is deep joy, spiritual celebration, a cause for blessing in our lives.

The difference between *negah* and *oneg* is where we put the *ayin*, the letter,

and where we put the *ayin*, our eyes.

The circle keeps turning,
and the gates offer continual entrances to Holy Healing.

Where will we put our eyes, our energy, our hearts, our faith?

How will we move from the end of affliction to the beginning of joy?

(Sources: *Sefer Yetzirah* 2:4, translation by Rabbi Jonathan Slater;

Rabbi Yitzhak Meir Rothenberg, the Gerer Rebbe on Leviticus 13:55)

Rabbi Debra Judith Robbins serves at Temple Emanu-El in Dallas, Texas, is a member of the seventh cohort of the IJS Rabbinic Leadership Program, a Hevraya participant, and a supporter of the IJS online daily meditation program.

She admires and appreciates Jonathan's extraordinary and humble generosity in sharing his Divine gifts of chochmah (wisdom), tevunah (skill) and da'at (interpretation) of every kind of sacred text, with all of us.

Metzora
Restoring the Soul's Companionship

Justin David

Metzora with its focus on Biblical leprosy seems so irrelevant, but as Rambam and the great Hasidic teachers remind us, it is all Torah. The *torat ha-metzora* is all about achieving a new connection to the Source of Life and its resonances amid human community and at the depths of one's being. For all of the attention the Torah devotes to the descriptions and consequences of *tzara'at*, it appears that the real focus is on the reintegration and the promise of new vitality for the *metzora*.

The ritual of return prompts one to consider the ways in which death and life, illness and healing all participate in a continuous flow. The re-integration ritual for the *metzora* appears so sensual, so replete with meaning, that it almost seems as if one should desire to be a *metzora*—if only to experience the transformation of coming back again. A kind of *yeridah l'tzorekh aliyah*. As the temporary alienation is inevitable, one may consider welcome the kind of experience from which to ascend anew.

The *piyyut*, *Yedid Nefesh*, places us in such an emotional space, that it prompts us to envision ourselves as outsiders yearning to be welcomed anew to the love garden of spiritual connection. Strikingly, there is a direct reference to Miriam's *tzara'at* when the poem quotes Moses' plea for her healing: *El na r' fa na la*. In the *piyyut's* mystical context, the associations lead one to a startling observation: our souls experience being a kind of *metzora* during the week. We are separated, through no fault of our own, from our spiritual source. By necessity, our attentions and energies drift from the root of our being. At the moment when we feel the distance and its yearning, we begin to feel the impulse to breathe differently, to sing, to cry out, to create. Shabbat - or any other reminder of the ever presence of love - offers a promise of our soul's return to new vitality.

Rabbi Justin David is spiritual leader of Congregation B'nai Israel in Northampton, MA and the author of Longing: Jewish Meditations on a Hidden God.

He blesses Jonathan with new vitality, especially among his circle of people who love him and to whom he has given so much and so deeply. Wishing you all joy in discovering new blessings!

Aharei Mot
Letting Go Into Our Deepest Self

K'vod Wieder

In *Aharei Mot*, we read about the very first Yom Kippur service as it took place in the *Mishkan* – the portable sanctuary. In that service, there was a life and death moment, when the *Kohen Gadol*, the high priest, would enter the Holy of Holies. He would somehow pronounce the unpronounceable name of God, and would invoke compassion and forgiveness from God to the entire people.

Knowing how the High Priest was able to be successful is key to understanding how we can grow and be a force for good in the world despite our imperfections. In our parsha, it says that no one was allowed in the inner courtyard when the High Priest went into the Holy of Holies. Rabbi Mordechai Yosef of Izbica (1801-1854) writes in his Torah commentary *Mei Hashiloach:*

And there shall be no man in the tent of meeting when he goes in to make atonement... (Lev 16:17)

"On the Day of Atonement, he enters beyond and within, which is a completely unique place. This is as it is written in the Holy Zohar (*Bemidbar* 130b), *for there are two nostrils, one draws in life, and the other draws in the life of all life.* With all of one's actions it is said, *the preparations of the heart are made by man, and the answer of the tongue is from God.* (Proverbs 16:1) Yet here it is different, as it is said, *and there shall be no man.*" When it comes to the service on the Day of Atonement and the effluence of Divine energy that flows at this time from the blessed God, there is absolutely no relevance to the self-concept of a person, in his thought or understanding.

Rabbi Mordechai Yosef is interpreting this verse to say that it doesn't just refer to a person not being allowed in the tent of meeting when the High Priest enters the Holy of Holies. It also refers to the High Priest, who has to enter without a concept of self- without any sense of identity, of role – without any judgments or ideas about the world, Israelites, or God – so that even "he" wasn't there. If he does that, the High Priest could pronounce the Infinite Holy Name of God without being destroyed. He and the rest of Israel were able to be transformed and forgiven.

Each one of us needs to have a time in our lives where we enter the Holy of Holies and not just on Yom Kippur. We need to have moments where we completely let go of everything we think we are and allow ourselves to be present with the infinite. Sometimes we can do that through letting go in prayer and song, sometimes in silence. Sometimes it can be a moment in a conversation, where we completely let go of our agenda, or the way we are used to perceiving the person in front of us, and instead just be totally open. Only when we give ourselves space to be released from our identity and ideas about ourselves and others, can we be open to compassion and forgiveness.

A practice:

Find a comfortable position and bring your awareness to the movement of breath. Become aware of your body in space – the shape of your body from the tip of your toes to the top of your head. Once your awareness is present with the moment to moment experience of body and breath, gently think the words, "not my body, not my breath, not my (whatever you are experiencing)." Be present to the unfolding experience of the moment without ownership. Consider that every part of your experience is an expression of Divine Presence.

Rabbi K'vod Wieder serves Temple Beth El of South Orange County and has taught meditation and Jewish spirituality for over 25 years.

He appreciates how Rabbi Jonathan's clear translations and commentaries make our early Hasidic textual traditions accessible and relevant for daily spiritual practice.

Kedoshim
Finding God, Finding Good; Hakarat Hatov

Molly Karp

Parashat Kedoshim is the heart of *Vayikra*, which is the heart of the Torah. It teaches us how to be holy, how to be like God – how to act and treat each other as made in the image of God. "You shall be holy, for I, YHVH your God, am holy." (19:2).

We are each made in God's image and contain a spark of the Divine. When we look at ourselves and each other-really look-we can see that spark. We contain and we are part of God. Seeing God in ourselves, in each other, leads us to see what is good in each person. In the words of Rabbi Nahman of Bratzlav, (Likutei Moharan 1:282)

You have to judge every person generously... it's your job to look hard and seek out some bit of goodness... When you find that bit of goodness, and judge that person that way, you may really elevate them to goodness...

My IJS teachers taught me to find the divine spark that is in myself and in others, to see myself as God might see me, and to see others as God would see them. I can act from a place of love rather than from a place of judgment. God is there for us to find, standing right in front of us, in ourselves and in each other. This practice of *hakkarat hatov* helps us to look for the good in ourselves, in each other, and in the world. This practice increases the good that is in the world, for as we seek good and find it, we actualize it and make the world better.

What is our practice? Seek the good in every person. Seek the good in every situation. In seeking and finding the good, we become more like God, and we can see God and the good in each other. This can bring us to the love that is at the heart of Torah and the heart of Jewish spirituality. It is the love that I learned at IJS, and from my IJS teachers.

Rabbi Molly Karp was a member of the Jewish Educators' cohort at IJS, and has participated in Hevraya since 2006. She works as a freelance

Rabbi, and as a Jewish educator, teaching a broad array of subjects to teens and adults in many venues. Her learning at IJS underpins all that she does.

What she loves about Jonathan is his ability to see God and the good in each of us, his deep love for the text and for us, his calm and loving acceptance of each of us as we are, and his lovingkindness in nurturing us into better versions of ourselves.

Emor
The Ground of Holiness Within

Lavey Yitzhak Derby

The fundamental mitzvah of *Kiddush Hashem*, the sanctification of God's name, derives from the verse "You shall not profane my holy name, that I may be sanctified in the midst of the Israelite people..." (Leviticus 22:32). Rabbinically, while the act of *Kiddush Hashem* refers to any public act that glorifies God, it is most often associated with martyrdom, and is referred to as *mesirat nefesh*, an act of self-sacrifice.

As is his practice, the Sefat Emet understands *ve'nikdashti*, "that I be sanctified", as an inner process: "The essence of holiness is found within Israel precisely, as our rabbis taught, 'a person should always see themself as if the Holy resides in their innards.' (Ta'anit 11a-b) This holiness cannot be found except through *mesirat nefesh*." (3:172)

What is the Holy that dwells within? It might be called soul, or our true nature, or the deep heart. It is the "Self" that is not bound by any story, image or thought. It is unbounded and infinite – *Ein Sof*, —a loving awareness in which we experience a profound sense of union with the One; a sense of existential stability, a groundless ground.

The Holy is discerning, but free of judgment. It is infinitely patient, kind, compassionate. It unconditionally loves what is. The Sefat Emet explains that to touch the inner place where *Ein Sof* dwells requires *mesirat nefesh*, the sacrifice of the ego. It requires that we let go of the conditioned mind and unconditionally accept all that arises.

Practice:

Find a posture that allows you to be both relaxed and alert. Feel the weight of the body on the seat.

Feel yourself grounded, held by the earth. Let your attention settle and begin to breathe from the abdomen. Rest in the breath and the subtle movements of the abdomen.

As sensations, emotions, and thoughts arise, if they are pleasant – note them and allow them to float out of your field of awareness.

Should bodily tension or ache, a reactive feeling, an invasive thought or unwelcome story arise, gently inquire of yourself – "can I accept this just as it is?" The egoic mind will likely answer "no." If this is what happens, ask yourself a slightly different question: "Is there a place within me that accepts this just as it is?"

The place within that unconditionally loves and accepts is the Holy.

Continue to practice in this way, for the duration of your meditation.

Rabbi Lavey Yitzhak Derby is the founder of Omek HaLev, and a teacher of meditation, Zohar, and Hasidic works.

He and Jonathan have known each other as teenagers at CampRamah, fwerewellow students at JTS, rabbinic colleagues in the San Francisco Bay Area, and friends in the first IJS rabbinic cohort. He is awed that, through it all, Jonathan has never ceased growing in wisdom and spiritual depth.

Behar
God at the Margins

Shayna De Lowe and Benjamin Spratt

Nested within the verses of *Parashat Behar*, we encounter the line: "But the land must not be sold beyond reclaim, for the land is Mine; you are but strangers resident with Me" (Lev. 25:23). The Hebrew hendiadys "גרים ותושבים" is one seen in many other moments in the Torah, a "resident stranger" being one not fully of the people but dwelling amongst them. The plain sense of this verse simply underscores the sense that we rent and God owns; no matter our status or privilege, at best we are all quasi-outsiders in place.

For Rabbi Moshe Chaim Ephraim, however, this initial reading misses an essential qualifier. The final word, עמדי, which is translated in the JPS as "with Me" may be better understood as "along with Me." That is, God is a resident stranger, and the observance of the jubilee year is a reminder that we, too, are resident strangers. In this radical reading, Ephraim notes the existential loneliness of God as mirroring our own - "for whomever is a stranger has no people with whom to cleave and to draw near and to tell of his experiences. And for anyone who's heart has no friend...when he sees a fellow stranger [and feels resonant as fellow outsiders] then he may recount with this person his experiences."[*] God exists alone and apart, without peer nor friend, without one to listen or bear witness. In being commanded to disrupt our own sense of belonging, we are invited to embrace a similar state of being, and as a fellow stranger, we may open ourselves better to being God's companion.

Ephraim is suggesting that in our own comfort and belonging, we often inadvertently abandon the outsider. Despite innumerable reminders to retain our awareness of being strangers, and therefore presumably being attuned to the strangers in our midst, here we are given a further impetus - without our own sense of solitude, we leave God alone and abandoned as well.

---

[*] *Degel Machaneh Ephraim*, Behar 1. Translation is our own.

For Rabbi Abraham Joshua Heschel, this was his entire frame of the purpose of *mitzvah* and prevention of sin. "The destiny of man is to be a partner of God and a *mitzvah* is an act in which man is present, an act of participation; while sin is an act in which God is alone; an act of alienation."** Commandment is a pathway for connection; sin is an act of abandonment.

Like so many of us, God too sits alone, searching for us in the wilderness of the world. In places of comfort, we forget our charge to embrace the outsider; in spaces of permanency, we forget the marginalized. If the primary purpose of *mitzvot* is connection, then it may be the most disruptive obligations, the burdens that expand perspective beyond comfort, that are most needed.

May we join God as resident strangers of this world, commanded to connect. And in the rhythms of relationship, disrupt ourselves enough to see God dwells not in the fortresses of steel and glass, but in the margins. In the heart of the stranger.

Rabbi Benjamin Spratt and Cantor Shayna De Lowe are the senior clergy of Congregation Rodeph Sholom in Manhattan. They were participants in the first cohort of the IJS Clergy Leadership Program and hold Jonathan as the teacher who gifted them with belonging, helping resident strangers find God in both the heart and the margins.

** *Between God and Man* (Free Press Paperbacks: New York, 1997), p. 80.

Behukotai
The Driven Leaf of our Life's Journey

Lorel Zar-Kessler

As for those you who survive, I will cast a faintness into their hearts in the land of their enemies. The sound of a driven leaf shall put them to flight. Fleeing as though from the sword, they shall fall through none pursues.
Lev. 26:36-37

This is amongst the most existential depictions within Torah. It is the sound of life's breath flailing and falling away. Nothing feels more real in human existence. It takes my breath away.

We are given gifts–that can feel so fragile as we choose to turn away from meaning and purpose, letting God's Presence slip away into alienation and emptiness. It happened to our ancestors, and in our world now, even after an evolution of guidance to keep us close to Godliness.

Yet, we have the gift of *teshuvah* that waits next to alienation. The Baal Shem Tov teaches, "we are insistently taught that *teshuvah*, return to God, really does work, and that the one who returns is fully renewed in God's presence. The task is to go forward, not interrupted by our own sense of inadequacy." (Arthur Green)

We become lost in a sea of enemies without, within, and yet, seven verses later:

"Even then, when they are in the land of their enemies, I will not reject them, annulling My covenant: for I YHVH am their God." (Lev. 26:44)

The Hasidic master, the Degel Machaneh Ephraim, applied the power of *teshuvah* to the dance of our lives: walking the path of coming closer to Godliness in our lives. He teaches that we feel pulled by God's gift of free will, which sometimes guides us in a 'straight path for Your Name's Sake," and sometimes pulls us far afield, path-less. We can see that straying as part of the path of our journey toward Godliness. We lose our way; we regain the compass direction – we zig or zag. The path is not linear; it is filled with both clarity and questioning. Still, we turn, and we see God's presence right before us. The covenant of *teshuvah* continually gives us an opportunity to come home, planted with our feet on the ground, our heads reaching toward the sky.

Walking Practice: Allow yourself to feel as 'a driven leaf' and also a grounded force.

WALK:
- Eyes closed and then open
- setting each step before you

Moving without direction
- watching the ground in front of you,

looking toward something yet unseen

Levi Yitzhak of Berdichev calls us to WALK in God's ways, both when we walk on a grounded path, and when we wander, toward an uncertain future. We continue to WALK in God's ways.

Cantor Lorel Zar-Kessler is Cantor Emerita, Congregation Beth El, Sudbury, MA.

She is a student of Jonathan Slater's masterful interpretations of our beloved Hasidic tradition. His teachings and his individual guidance are gifts to us all.

Bemidbar
Uplifting Our Pilot Light

Marc Margolius

As *Bemidbar* begins, the Israelites prepare to leave Mt. Sinai and resume their journey through the wilderness. Moses readies them by taking a census of males able to bear arms. Strikingly, in describing the process of counting, the Torah employs language connoting "lifting" (Numbers 1: 1-4):

> YHVH spoke to Moses in the wilderness of Sinai, in the tent of meeting, on the first day of the second month in the second year after they had come out of the land of Egypt, saying: 'Take the sum [*se'u et ro*sh, literally: "lift the head"] of all the community of the Children of Israel, according to their families, their father's households, counting [*be-mispar*] the names of the men by their heads, from 20 years old and up, all in Israel able to go forth to war: number them by their hosts, you and Aaron.'

A Hasidic interpretation of this passage by Rabbi Yosef Bloch (1860-1929), author of *Ginzei Yosef*, assigns special significance to the use of the term *se'u*, "lift:"

> The real counting of Israel points upward, toward their Root above. The six hundred thousand Israelite souls have their source in the six *sefirot* [from *chesed* to *yesod*], the "six directions." That's why the text says "lift up the head" and not simply "count." This act of Moses's counting awakened the light of that Source, shining down brightly upon Israel. It raised them up to the highest rungs of awe and love, directing their hearts to the ever-present God. ... This is **"Lift up the head:"**

raise Israel to its highest Root. "**According to their Father's household**" [means] the Source of their souls. [Be-mispar] means shining. "**The names**," for a person's name represents the life-force within. Thus, the light of their upper Source comes to shine within them, each according to their name or essential flow of life.

To "count" individuals is to link all souls with their deepest roots, the sacred qualities from which they emerge. Our ability to recognize and cultivate the innate goodness in each soul, including our own, guides us on our individual and collective life journeys.

We can practice this teaching at any moment: simply bring attention to each inhalation as it arises, imagining the oxygen it holds sustaining your "inner pilot light," your connection to the Source of Life, fanning that light so that its sacred qualities shine brightly within your being. With each exhalation, allow that light to flow into the world as the highest expression of your "name," your utterly unique, precious manifestation of the Divine.

Rabbi Marc Margolius is a Senior Program Director with the Institute for Jewish Spirituality, and a fellow member, with Jonathan, of IJS's inaugural rabbinic cohort.

He is ever-grateful to Jonathan for enabling him to see the deeper dimensions of Torah, and for his example of pausing to reflect on the wisdom of whether and how to choose to act or speak so as to add to – and not detract from – the holiness of life.

Naso
Awakening to God's Protection and Presence

Ilene Berns-Zare & Toby Hayman

Naso contains three verses among the most familiar in Jewish life — *Birkat Kohanim* —the Priestly Blessings (Numbers 6:22-26). These blessings invite us to mindfully and deeply experience the whole truth of our connection to YHVH.

The Torah tells us "I will bless them" (6:27). God instructs the *kohanim* to speak the words aloud to the people of Israel, who are blessed by YHVH. In contemporary Judaism, whether offered by *kohen*, rabbi, parent, loved one, or friend, the blessings revitalize our awareness of God's protection and presence. As we pray, we listen for the Holy Voice, the presence of divine love and goodness. God's face is lifted toward us and peace is renewed וְיָשֵׂם לְךָ שָׁלוֹם. We are lifted as we draw nearer to our Source in the light of *shalom* —wholeness and fulfillment. Our spiritual wellsprings are activated, deepening mindfulness, compassion, and love, inviting us to carry our awakened vitality into daily life, thought, and action.

Are we fully present to the lovingkindness that is our inheritance? What is our *kavvanah* – our intention?

Levi Yitzhak of Berdichev taught that blessings come through us, not from us, and that our prayers bring joy to the Creator. YHVH is the source from which blessings emanate. *Chiyut* – the river of lifeforce energy — emanates from the Holy Blessed One as the love of creation flows through the core of our beings.

When we offer God's blessings to each other, we are also praying for and blessing ourselves. It is an embodied practice infusing our minds, physical bodies, and spirits. As we pronounce the words and rest in the quiet space between them, we're enlivened by our strivings to know our deep connection with God and the lifeforce energies that sustain us. We're partners with the Holy Blessed One, praying with the implicit hope that YHVH is listening. We speak the words aloud desiring to know that YHVH joins with us in divine delight, abundant with holy sparks, and a deep river of protection, grace, and peace.

Birkat Kohanim offers a fountain flowing with spiritual renewal, where humans and our Creator are one. The blessings invite us to care for each other and all humanity. Our hearts and souls are awakened as we speak the prayers and receive them in partnership with our Source. The Divine gift, to bless and be blessed, is true in each moment of our lives, as the letters and words of Torah illuminate our souls.

Dr. Ilene Berns-Zare was a member of the IJS Wise Aging cohort and has studied virtually with Rabbi Jonathan in Torah study, mindfulness sits, and his writings. Ilene is inspired by Jonathan, treasuring his teachings and thankful for his guidance as she aspires to be fully present to the truths of each moment.

Hazzan Toby Lou Hayman is a Spiritual Director and the Spiritual Leader of Chicago's Central Synagogue. She has been Rabbi Jonathan's student since the first Cantorial Leadership Program offered by IJS. He is a treasured teacher, who has guided her realization, experience, and connection to the Presence of the Divine and these blessings in every moment.

Beha'alotekha
Lift up the Lights

Laura Geller

Our Torah portion begins with God's instruction to Moses: "Speak to Aaron and say to him, "When you mount the lamps, let the seven lamps give light at the front of the lampstand. And Aaron did so."

The seven branched menorah is perhaps the most fundamental of Jewish symbols. Why is the menorah so central?

Is it just that it is so ancient, that it was part of the portable tabernacle we carried with us 3000 years ago? Is it that our tradition tells us that the pattern of the menorah was given to God by Moses at Mt Sinai? Is it that Jewish mysticism teaches that the menorah is a symbol of the seven dimensions of God we can experience in our lives, or that the oil is divine energy flowing through the branches to each of us? Or is it, as hasidic teachers suggest, that the light of the menorah is a glimpse of the primordial light that existed the first week of creation before the creation of the sun and moon, a light that offers us the ability to see more clearly what is true? Is it that the menorah comes to represent the Temple, a holy place, or any place where we can connect with Divinity? Or is it that the menorah evokes the tree of life as it must have looked to Adam and Eve from outside Eden?

"So YHVH Elohim banished the human from the garden of Eden, to till the soil from which he was taken. God drove the human out, and stationed east of the garden of Eden the cherubim and the fiery ever-turning sword, to guard the way to the tree of life." (Gen.3:23,24)

Imagine them, the first human beings, standing outside, east of Eden, looking back through the fire of the ever-turning sword guarded by the cherubim. Imagine them wanting to return to the garden, to the tree of life. And now imagine yourself looking at the fire of a seven branched menorah, looking through it to a tree of life, a burning bush. Imagine looking toward a connection to Divinity still accessible to us where we are at this moment, east of Eden, in the real world of our real lives. Focusing on our breath connects us to that divine energy flowing through those branches into us.

Rabbi Laura Geller, Rabbi Emerita of Temple Emanuel of Beverly Hills, is the co-author with Richard Siegel (z'l) of Getting Good at Getting Older.

Rabbi Jonathan Slater was in that first cohort of rabbis at the IJS that changed my life and opened her heart. Jonathan has embodied the commandment not just to light the lights but to lift up the lights of the menorah, to make it visible to other people so it continues. Like Aaron in our Torah portion, Jonathan did so. And she will be forever grateful.

Shelach Lekha
The Landscape of Your Life

Laura Hegfield

In *Parashat Shelach Lekha*, Moses sends one man from each tribe to "see the land what is it?" *ur'item et ha'aretz mah hee...* (Numbers 13:8) Although they saw a land flowing with milk and honey, fear caused them to embellish their report, saying that the people in the land were giants, and that the Israelites were like grasshoppers in comparison.

Later, God tells Moshe: "Speak to the Israelites— instruct them to make *tzitzit* on the corners of their clothes throughout the generations; have them attach a cord of blue to the *tzitzit* at each corner. *V'hayah lakhem l'tzitzit ur'item oto uzkhartem et kol mitzvot Adonai* This is your *tzitzit*; You shall see it [*ur'item oto*] and remember all the *mitzvot* of God and do them, *velo taturu acharei levavkhem ve'acharey eineikhem* so that you are not be led astray by the desires of your heart/mind and eyes, so you remember to do all my *mitzvot* and be holy for your God." (Numbers 15: 38-40)

Tzitzit remind us to be mindful, to see what it true, through the natural inclinations of heart and mind that lead us astray like the spies. Layers of worry, planning, confusion, and fear entangle us in stories around what is true moment to moment. *"Ur'item et ha'aretz mah hee*, see the land what is it? The actual landscape of your life; *"ur'item oto* see it."

The *Sefat Emet** teaches *"ur'item oto,"* is read by the Sages to mean that you shall see God's presence, for 'Whoever fulfills the commandment of the *tzitzit* merits greeting the *Shekhinah.*'1 Thus we may look at the glory of God's kingdom, which exists in every thing, as it says: 'The whole earth is full of God's glory, (Is. 6:3). But it is hidden, and a truly wholehearted act of self-negation allows one to see God's shining glory.'

Ur'item oto, seeing "it", comes through lived experience; interactions

---

* *The Language of Truth: The Torah Commentary of the Sefat Emet, Rabbi Yehudah Leib Alter of Ger*, Arthur Green, p. 239

with people, the natural world, observing our innermost thoughts, sensations, and emotions. As the Sefat Emet taught, we must engage in a "wholehearted act of self-negation." Thoughts and emotions arise all the time, creating a kind of subterfuge, hiding the truth that is present and visible, *ur'item oto*.

In addition to wearing a *tallit* or *tallit katan*, mindful breath can be a sign, like *tzitzit*; whenever you realize you are caught in a story, let your breath be a sign, guiding you back to what is happening now, to see the truth of each moment arising exactly as "it" is.

Laura Hegfield is a longtime Hevraya member and Jewish heart-mindfulness educator in New Hampshire.

What she loveslove about Jonathan, beyond his brilliant translations and interpretations of Torah, is that he infuses everything he offers and each personal encounter with love, curiosity, wisdom and kind attention; his gentle, attentive presence alone is a "teaching."

Korah
We are All Holy

Seth Goldstein

"You have gone too far! For all the community are holy,
all of them, and God is in their midst. Why then do you
raise yourselves above God's congregation?" (Numbers
16:3)

With these words Korah challenged Moses's authority and leadership over the Israelite community, creating a moment of instability and uncertainty in the governance of the people.

Regardless of what we think of Korah and his campaign, there is an element in these words that resonate with us. We like to think that everyone is holy—or has the potential for holiness—it is a foundational Jewish value informing our interpersonal relationships.

Later in the story, Moses himself makes this claim. After Korah's initial challenge, Moses summons Dathan and Aviram, who side with Korah. They refuse to come, claiming that Moses brought the Israelites into the wilderness out of a land of plenty (Egypt) and had not brought them to a Promised Land. Most of all, Moses *tistarer aleynu* "lords it over" the people.

In response, a distraught Moses turns to God and says, "Pay no regard to their oblation. I have not taken the ass of any one of them, nor have I wronged any one of them." (Numbers 16:15)

In reflecting on Moses's response, the Kedushat Levi writes,

The general rule is that that Moses constantly tried to
spiritually uplift the people of Israel and to thereby bring
them closer to him. He states here that this endeavor of
his included every single one of the Israelites. He did not
elevate a single Israelite at the expense of others whom
he did not elevate. Similarly, when trying to be close to
the people, he did not favor any Israelite at the expense
of another Israelite about whom he supposedly cared less.

In other words, it is not only that Moses did not oppress anyone (as the Torah says), but he actively tried to elevate each individual Israelite spiritually and draw close to each individual Israelite emotionally.

Moses recognized that the need for a leader, or a teacher, or a mentor, is not mutually exclusive with Korah's claim that "all the community is holy." In fact, a good leader agrees with Korah and sees all those under their charge as equal, taking interest in and attending to each and every person. In any occasion in which we find ourselves in such a position, we should strive to do the same.

Practice:
Combine the words of Korah and the intention of Moses. In preparation for a meeting or an appointment with another person, repeat the words from Numbers "kol ha'edah kulam kedoshim," and think how you can contribute to the elevation of that person. This can be done during the interaction as well, especially if it is a difficult one. Alternatively, you can use these words as a meditation while out in public—on a plane, or in a supermarket—in order to cultivate generosity of spirit and favorable judgment towards others.

Rabbi Seth Goldstein, is the rabbi of Temple Beth Hatfiloh in Olympia, WA.

In his view, Jonathan embodied the spirit of Moses as described above, and he felt special and uplifted in his presence during his time in the IJS Clergy Leadership Program.

Chukkat
Each According to their Soul

David Ackerman

Commanded to speak to the rock so that it will produce water, Moses instead strikes the rock with his staff. Abundant water flows but there's a grave consequence for Moses: "Because you did not trust Me enough to affirm My sanctity before the eyes of the Israelite people, therefore you shall not lead this congregation into the land that I have given them." (Numbers 20:12)

What misstep warrants such a severe outcome? Summarizing Rashi's comment on our verse, Aviva Zornberg observes that speaking rather than hitting "would have produced a thoughtful response in the people...they would have come to recognize the power of God's word in their own vulnerable and dependent lives."

R. Avraham Dov of Avritch (19th century Ukraine/Tzefat) pursues a similar line. "It was for you to sanctify Me and to have faith that I welcome repenters...it was for you to reinforce the attribute of *hesed* — of course the blemish can be repaired!" (*Bat Ayin, Chukkat*)

Moses missed an opportunity to engage in holistic, people-centered, spiritual leadership, a mode of leadership that R. Avraham Dov himself described in one of my very favorite Hasidic texts:

So, too, here: because they are "Your children", with refined sensibilities, no one's mind is like another, and they are demanding of one another. Therefore, appoint over them a leader who can bear each one according to their character. This is the simple meaning.

But, in truth, this is the explanation: no one's mind is like another, as each one was created to serve God in a different manner, according to their soul. This is as the holy teacher R. Yaakov Yitzhak, the *Chozeh* of Lublin taught: each and every person was created for a different service. After all, if this one was created for this service, why would another also be created — it must be for some other service!

The leader, i.e., the *rebbe*, must know the souls of each and every one, and know the service that pertains to that soul, and to draw them near and connect them to their root-source.

This is what it means: appoint a leader who can bear each one according to their character, i.e., their soul, to draw them near and connect them to their root-source, each and every one according to their soul. [*Sefer Bikkurei Aviv, Pinchas,* translation: R Jonathan Slater]

Moses missed the mark at Meribah. We who play leadership roles are called to hit it daily.

Picture a crowd of people in front of you. Perhaps you're attending a concert, or walking down a busy street, or sitting in synagogue...Take a deep breath and look again at the crowd. Don't count or estimate their number. Rather, consider that each one is a unique soul, here to serve God in their own unique fashion. Take another deep breath. And now look more closely at one or two of the individual souls arrayed before you. Can you come to know that soul deeply, 'draw them near,' and then 'connect them to their root-source?'

Rabbi David Ackerman serves as spiritual leader at Congregation Beth Am Israel in Penn Valley, PA.

He admires and adores his teacher, mentor, and guide Rabbi Jonathan Slater for his intellect, heart, and gentle wisdom.

Balak
Love, No Matter the Spelling

Darren Kleinberg

The Apter Rov, Rabbi Abraham Joshua Heschel (1748 – 1825), was also known as the *Ohev Yisrael*, the lover of the Jewish people. According to tradition, he gained this appellation because every shabbat he would give a *shi'ur*/talk and connect the weekly parashah to the theme of *ahavat Yisrael*, in particular, and also *ahavat hab'riyot*/love of all creatures, more generally.

One Shabbat during the summer months, the hasidim came to shul to hear the Rebbe's *shi'ur*, feeling quite confident that there was no way he could possibly link that week's portion– *parashat Balak* – to the theme of loving Jews. Let alone all of creation.

And so, they sat in their seats, facing the Rebbe, with looks on their faces that said "*nu? vus kennen ir machen fun eym?/*"show us what you can do." Clearly perceiving the crafty looks on the faces of the hasidim, the Rebbe said: "of all the *parshiyot*, this is the one that teaches the mitzvah of 'loving your neighbor as yourself' better than any other!" The hasidim were stunned. "How could it be? The story of *parashat Balak* is about an attempt to curse the Jewish people. Where, in this strangest of *parshiyot* could 'loving your neighbor as yourself' possibly be found?!," they wondered to themselves.

With a wise and crafty smile on his face, the Rebbe gently said: "*Pshita!* Simple, it's in the *roshei teivot*" (acrostic). The hasidim all tilted their heads at the same time, confounded by the Rebbe's words, but no-one dared say anything.

Again, the Rebbe said, "It's in the *roshei teivot*" this time adding: "*Balak: Beit. Lamed. Kuf.*" Even more confused than before, the hasidim tilted their heads further, almost popping them off their necks.

Finally, the Rebbe said, "*Beit. Lamed. Kuf. Ve'ahavta le'reyeicha kamokha! Pshita!*"—Love your neighbor as yourself.

The hasidim could no longer contain themselves. In unison, they said, "But Rebbe! *Balak* is spelled *beit, lamed, kuf,* and the *roshei teivot* of *ve'ahavta le'reyeicha kamokha* are *vav, lamed, khaf*! What do you mean 'It's in the *roshei teivot*'?!"

To which the Rebbe responded gently, "you see, that's the point, *mein kinder*; when it comes to loving your neighbor, there's no need to be picky about the spelling."

Rabbi Darren Kleinberg is Dean of the Aleph Ordination Program.
He shares this story in honor of his teacher, Rabbi Jonathan Slater, who, in his experience, is never picky about the spelling when it comes to loving others.

Pinhas
Leadership and Listening
A Communal Spiritual Practice

Eric Rosin

In a powerful moment in *Parashat Pinhas*, God tells Moses that the end of Moses' life is approaching and that he will not live to lead his people into the Land of Israel.

Remarkably, Moses' response is not to question God's judgment (although he will do so elsewhere in the Torah and the rabbis of the midrash will amplify those protests eloquently). Instead, in this passage Moses petitions God to select another leader to take his place, someone who will "go out before the Israelites and come in before them." In a moment that would have been a personal crisis for a lesser person, Moses teaches us that, leadership is not embodied in any particular person. Leadership is an ongoing spiritual practice.

This point is further clarified in the specific language that God uses to respond to Moses' appeal. According to the New Jewish Publication Society translation of the Torah, God answers, "Single out Joshua son of Nun, an inspired man and lay your hand upon him." (Numbers 27:18)

The Hebrew is even more evocative. What JPS translates as "an inspired man," the text of the Torah sets forth as *ish asher ruach bo*, a man within whom there is *ruach*, spirit.

Rabbi Hayyim Ephraim of Sudilkov in his commentary, the *Degel Machaneh Ephraim* clarifies further. He teaches that God singles out Joshua because Joshua is the kind of leader who can perceive and hold the thoughts of each member of the community, even when those thoughts are many and varied and in conflict with one another. In this way, the *Degel* teaches, a leader becomes "the collective thought of all Israel, and all of them will be present in him, each one according to his or her thoughts." (Adapted from the translation of Rabbi Jonathan Slater.)

The spiritual practice of leading emerges from a teaching of the

Ba'al Shem Tov. When speaking to others, a leader attaches his or herself to the will of our creator. When listening to others a true leader can hear the divine voice speaking through them.

Practice:
This practice cannot be followed in isolation. In order to enter into this understanding of leadership, one must be in relationship to another.

Take a moment at the beginning of your day and sit quietly, feet flat on the floor, finding your breath.

When you have settled, think forward into the day to come and choose a moment when you will be in relationship with another person, perhaps a member of your family or someone with whom you work or even someone whom you don't know well and set the intention to be fully present in that relationship.

Commit to listening to what is said, and to being curious about what the other person is experiencing. Be careful with your responses. Craft your words in such a way that they embody God's love for the other person.

Allow yourself to explore the question: What does this moment in the relationship ask of me?

Rabbi Eric Rosin has been a pulpit rabbi for 20 years. He and his hevruta, Susanne Singer, have been learning with Jonathan's texts weekly for over a decade. Eric is immeasurably grateful for the way that Jonathan's teachings have opened up the world of Hasidut to him and is no less grateful for Jonathan's counsel and friendship.

Mattot
Our Words Are Wondrously Holy And Transformative

SaraLeya Schley

אִישׁ כִּי־יִדֹּר נֶדֶר לַיהֹוָה אוֹ־הִשָּׁבַע שְׁבֻעָה לֶאְסֹר אִסָּר עַל־נַפְשׁוֹ לֹא יַחֵל דְּבָרוֹ כְּכָל־הַיֹּצֵא מִפִּיו יַעֲשֶׂה:

One who vows a vow to YHVH or swears an oath that binds oneself to a prohibition must not violate/desecrate/profane one's words – exactly what comes out of the mouth, one must do. (Numbers 30:3)

Rebbe Nosson (Likutei Halakhot Birkhot HaShahar 5:90) and Rebbe Nahman (Likutei Moharan 57:2) speak of the wondrous potential of acts of speech, especially vows, to unleash the creative wisdom of the soul. A vow of abstention sanctifies us by limiting our behavioral choices, in essence creating for ourselves a new personal mitzvah.

Both the *Sefat Emet* and the *Netivot Shalom* begin with Rashi's interpretation of the verb יַחֵל in our source verse as "do not make your words commonplace – לא יעשה דבריו חולין", with the word *hullin* in rabbinic parlance being the opposite of holy.

The *Sefat Emet*, R. Yehuda Leib Alter of Gur teaches that speech has the potential of holiness and thus Torah instructs us in *sh'mirat ha-lashon*/ monitoring our speech. Speech is related to prayer, our substitute for the sacrificial system. The voice of prayer is unbounded (בלי מצרים); via our speech we make vows in times of difficulty. During difficult times (בין המצרים – as during The Three Weeks is when *Mattot* is read), we strengthen and rectify our voice of Torah and prayer to experience freedom and relief. His conclusion reminds us that the potential of the mouth is unlocked through the holiness of the soul, וע"י קדושת הנשמה נפתח כח הפה, perhaps alluding to the identification of speech with *shekhinah*, the indwelling Divine Presence, thus infusing voice with sacredness.

The Slonimer Rebbe, in his opus the *Netivot Shalom*, notes how a vow changes the essence of a matter by a mere act of speech:

> By speaking about a matter, it is changed from its current reality and a new reality takes effect – that of something either forbidden or dedicated to Divine service.

He cites Rabeinu Yonah's comments on Pirkei Avot 1:17 that our Sages would make themselves vessels of Temple service by not trivializing their speech. When one's mouth becomes a vessel for holy service it has the unique potential to transform all one's limbs to a state of *kedushah*/holiness appropriate for Divine service. Finally, he discussed the Zohar's assertion of the creative power of holy words – creating and renewing worlds, heaven, earth and person.

Practice:
These three Hasidic masters bring us 3 different aspects of the importance of mindful speech:

From the Bratzlaver tradition, we ask are we willing to use this transformative power to create for ourselves new behavioral expectations?

From the *Sefat Emet*, we are assured that words of Torah and prayer have the potential to release us from our constrictions and troubles; however, as we meditate with discernment, we ask how and whether this assertion brings us comfort and/or challenge.

Finally, the *Netivot Shalom* teaches that our mouths have the power to be a vessel of Divine service that can lead us to realizing our creative potential for renewal. We might consider a daily practice of reviewing our speaking and how our relative proportion of ordinary speech is balanced with our words of prayer, study, comfort and other mitzvot such as rebuke.

Rabbi SaraLeya Schley, currently resides in Sparks (Nitzotzot) NV, and teaches Integral Halakha for the Aleph Ordination Program, and is a long-term devotee of the study of Kabbalah and Hasidut. She has valued Jonathan's mentorship and guidance since her participation in the fifth cohort the IJS Rabbinic Leadership Program and through his years of IJS weekly Hasidic parshanut.

Mas'ei
The Forty-Two Journeys of Your Life

Naomi Levy

Parashat Mas'ei includes a list of all the places in the wilderness our ancestors journeyed through on their way to the Promised Land. The list is long and seems irrelevant. The locations don't exist on any map today. They don't point us in any direction. What can such a list possibly come to teach us?

The *Netivot Shalom* insists that this boring list is one of the holiest sections of the Torah. He quotes the Besht, who taught that this laundry list of places is actually a blueprint for your life. The forty-two stops our ancestors made on their journey teaches us that each one of us must pass through forty-two journeys in our lifetime from birth to that final journey.

Every phase of your life, every place you've lived, every relationship you've been in, every loss, every birth, every success, every heartbreak – all of them have been quietly leading you forward. Every experience presents us with a twofold holy mission: to lift something up, and to learn.

Sometimes we look at our lives and we see a bunch of stops and starts that don't seem to add up to much of anything. But we couldn't be more mistaken. Every place we've been through in our lives has been our teacher.

Every encounter we have, no matter how fleeting, is an invitation for us to touch someone else in a world that is starved for connection. Sometimes we think we've taken a wrong turn, or worse, we feel utterly stalled and paralyzed. This pandemic has caused most of us to feel stuck and alone. But the *Netivot Shalom*, quoting Rashi, insists that even our stops are journeys! **There's no need to beat yourself up for the setbacks—love and learn, that's the key.** Like a flower bulb beneath parched land your soul has been waiting for the moment to break through and bloom.

What step are you on right now of the forty-two journeys of your life? Everything has led you to where you are right now. May you uncover your mission in every place and may you live to fulfill it, Amen.

Practice:

On the cover of a journal write: "My Forty-Two Journeys." Now begin. Ask yourself: *What are the journeys I've been through in my life? Where have I been and who have I been with? Can I see what was needed from me? What have I given, how have I contributed? Who taught me? What have I learned? What turns do I view as mistakes? What holy sparks can I glean from those very mistakes? What have been my celebrations? And how closely do I treasure those moments? How often do I turn to them for strength and comfort? Where have I been stalled? Where am I now?*

Each day ask: *What can I learn today* and *What can I give?* Let them become your morning mantra. Each night ask, *what did I learn today? How did I contribute?* And most importantly, *how can I build on these lessons tomorrow?*

Higher and Higher!

Rabbi Naomi Levy is the spiritual leader of Nashuva in Los Angeles and she is the author of To Begin Again, Talking to God, Hope Will Find You *and* Einstein and the Rabbi.

Jonathan has taught her that every word of Torah is waiting to whisper its wisdom to our souls, and through us, to our world.

.

Devarim
To Take the Next Step

Cindy Enger

Parashat Devarim begins a series of farewell addresses in which Moses prepares the Israelite people to cross over into the promised land at last. After multiple missteps and failures of faith, gluttonous cravings and frequent complaints, how will our Israelite ancestors muster the courage to move forward now without Moses?

Though this is a new generation, one born in the wilderness and not as slaves in Egypt, it is by no means a given that they will meet the challenges of this moment of transition. Moses must know this, and his opening words offer them guidance. "The Eternal our God spoke to us at Horeb, saying: 'You have stayed long enough at this mountain. *P'nu u'seu lakhem.* Start out and make your way… Go, take possession of the land…'" (Deut. 1:6-8).*

Interestingly, the prod to leave Horeb/Sinai does not appear in the Torah's first four books. In speaking these words of purported retrospective, Moses words are actually generative: *P'nu u'seu lakhem — turn yourselves and journey on.* This is a two-part process.

When courage is called for, an inner readying must precede taking any external first step. This is *p'nu.* It is this turning inward and facing the interior landscape with all of its texture and truths—fear and doubt, compassion and forgiveness, excitement and joy — that readies our Israelite ancestors to take their next step.

Moses spoke these words to our ancestors as they prepared to cross over into the promised land. He likely intended the teaching for himself as well, aware of the courage called for in crossing the threshold from this world to whatever comes next. And Moses is speaking to each of us, as inheritors of the tradition and contemporary readers of the Torah text. We read this Torah portion each year on

---

* *P'nu u'seu lakhem….* "Start out and make your way" might also be translated as "turn yourselves and journey" or "face about, march on." See, e.g, *The Torah with Rashi's Commentary* (Artscroll Saperstein Edition) and Everett Fox, *The Five Books of Moses.*

Shabbat Hazon just before Tisha Be-Av, the low point of the Jewish year when structures shatter and exile is felt within. The process of *teshuvah*/repentance calls for courage. Moses' words, *p'nu u'seu lakhem,* teach us how to begin.

Practice:
Sit comfortably and take several full breaths. Bring attention to your body, feeling the sensations in your heart center and in your belly, not forcing anything, simply noticing what is.

Ask yourself: what is my next step? Turn inward to observe without judgment the inner landscape. Try to name the sensations that are arising. Bring a hand to your heart, tending to yourself with lovingkindness. What prayer might you offer as you prepare to take the next step?

Rabbi Cindy Enger participated in the sixth cohort of the IJS Rabbinic Leadership Program and the second cohort of the IJS Jewish Mindfulness Teacher Training.

She has deep respect for Rabbi Jonathan Slater's scholarship and appreciation for his kindness and sense of humor.

Va'etchanan
The Grace of an Unanswered Prayer

Jamie Gibson

Although *Va'etchanan* contains two of the most famous passages in all Jewish sacred text, the Ten Commandments and Shema/*V'ahavata*, it is worth exploring the meaning of the portion's first word: Va'etchanan.

The reflexive form of the verb based on the root *ch–n–n*, "to plead or seek grace" for oneself. In our portion, Moshe says to our people, "*Va'etchanan el YHVH ba'eit ha'hi lei-mor…I pleaded with God at that time, saying…*" (Deuteronomy 3.23)

Chen means "grace," or the consideration that God gives us that we have not earned. The unearned gift that Moshe is asking for is to be allowed into the Promised Land after striking the rock at the waters of Meribah. (Numbers 20.10-13)

God rejects Moshe's plea and admonishes him never to mention it again. We might think, if Moshe's prayer is rejected out of hand, what chance do **our** prayers have of being accepted by God?

The Ishbitzer Rebbe, in his work *Mei HaShiloach*, writes about Moshe's pleading:

> *Why did Moshe Rabbenu tell these words to Israel? Even though on the surface it seems as if his prayer had no benefit whatsoever, nonetheless, he caused them to understand that his prayer was not in vain…)*

How was Moshe's prayer not in vain if his plea was not granted? The Ishbitzer continues:

> *(It is as if he is saying to them] even in the course of actions in the land of Israel I am your teacher and Rabbi, and likewise God showed them that his prayer was effective. This is why* Va'etchanan, *Hebrew for "and I pleaded" because*

he was made full of entreatment for God's mercies, *and his prayer flowed naturally from his mouth. This is a kind of proof that* God sent him the awakening *from below to pray. Therefore, he surely would not be turned away empty-handed. This is hinted at by "at that time," for even though God had already promised that I would not enter the land,* still it did not prevent me from praying... Even though it may seem that there is no salvation from the source, one may not withhold himself from God's mercies.

It seems that the Ishbitzer is teaching that we should not focus on the outcome of our prayers, rather on our capacity to pray in the first place. He teaches that the connection we achieve with God by actually opening ourselves to prayer is more valuable than any particular outcome, great or small, for which we are praying.

Even when Moses knew his request would not be answered favorably, he still was able to pray. He prayed for God's mercies rather than for God to change God's mind.

May we, who open our hearts and plead to God, pray for God's mercies rather than God's actions on our behalf. If we do, our prayers, like Moshe's, will never be in vain.

Rabbi Jamie Gibson is the Emeritus Rabbi of Temple Sinai in Pittsburgh, PA, where he served for 32 years. He is a Senior Rabbinic Fellow of the Shalom Hartman Institute and a member of the sixth cohort of the IJS Rabbinic Leadership Program.

Jonathan Slater and his teaching have inspired him for the last 13 years. His devotion to both the letter and spirit of Hasidic text lifted his spirit during challenges in his professional and personal life. He is indebted to Jonathan for his keen mind, his open heart and his accepting spirit.

Ekev
Eat, Fill, Bless

Dorothy Richman

וְאָכַלְתָּ וְשָׂבָעְתָּ וּבֵרַכְתָּ אֶת־יְהוָה אֱלֹהֶיךָ עַל־הָאָרֶץ הַטֹּבָה אֲשֶׁר
נָתַן־לָךְ:

And when you eat and are satisfied, you are to bless
YHWH your God for the good land that God has given
you. (Deut 8:10 - amended Everett Fox translation).

The Maggid of Mezritch was visited by a wealthy man. The Maggid
asked him: What do you eat every day? The wealthy man responded
that he ate like a poor person: bread dipped in salt. The Maggid
rebuked him, and ordered the wealthy man to eat meat and drink
honey mead every day in the way that the wealthy are accustomed.

After the wealthy man left, the Maggid's students asked him why
he had ordered the man to do this. The Maggid responded: This
wealthy man— if he eats meat every day and drinks honey mead—
will know that a poor person needs at least to eat some bread dipped
in salt. But if he eats bread dipped in salt each day, he will think that
a poor person needs to eat stones. (*The Stories of the Hasidim*, Shlomo
Yosef Zavin, Israel, 2000)

Eating is so complicated.

How beautiful the simplicity of the verse in Deuteronomy: Eat,
be full, bless.

And yet.

For many of us, eating becomes a minefield of difficult experiences:
Am I eating too much? Am I allowed to have this? Am I being good?

The Maggid's story emphasizes the way that eating can affect our
self-concept and our way of interacting with others. Here, a wealthy
man "plays" at being poor by eating as if he couldn't afford better. The
Maggid's rebuke shows that the wealthy man's self-denial was not
an expression of solidarity with the poor, nor did it lead to empathy

or generosity.

The Maggid orders the wealthy man to consume meat and mead because he knows that people respond more compassionately from abundance. Considering Deuteronomy's recipe for a meal: to eat, be satisfied, and bless— many of us are lucky to have regular access to healthy food and the knowledge to bless after we eat. But what do we know about feeling satisfied?

This may be a practice question— one to engage with over and over again. The practice of asking— what does fullness feel like right now in my body? What are the sensations of satisfaction? This may be a practice for each stage of a meal.

V'akhalta: eat with awareness and attention to flavor, to pleasure, to the body's responses. *V'savata:* Ask the question: Am I full? Is there abundance here? How can I share?

Uverakhta: Bless with gratitude for the land and the food and all those who helped grow, package, transport and prepare it.

May we bless and share our blessings.

Rabbi Dorothy Richman teaches Torah and other spiritual practices.
Rabbi Jonathan Slater's generosity as a teacher and mentor is, in itself, a blessing of abundance.

Shoftim
Give Voice to Their Name

Susan Leider

What's in a name? Who is a name for?

In Judaism, God's proper name is YHVH, as the psalmist says, "YHVH is Your name forever (*l'olam*), (Ps. 135:13).

The letters YHVH convey the eternal sense of being that goes beyond time and space as we know it. The sacred letters remind us that our very existence is grounded in this gift of being. Yet we know that the presence of the Divine goes beyond any proper name. The Zohar teaches that without this life force granted to us, that every Name in our universe would be like a body without a soul (Tikunei Zohar 17b). The name of the Divine makes it possible for all of us to have a name.

The *Or Ha Me'ir*, Ze'ev Wolf of Zhitomir, teaches in the name of the Baal Shem Tov, that we should read Psalm 135:13 this way: "YHVH is your name for the **world** (*l'olam*)." Not only can the Hebrew world "*olam*" mean "forever," but it can also mean "world." When we call out to the Divine using the name YHVH, it is for the sake of all human beings.

How do we thoughtfully practice this teaching of the *Or Ha Me'ir*? How do we help to create a spiritual reality that embodies that the Divine name is for the whole world? We do this by acknowledging others in the world and by voicing their names **as they best understand them**. While we often call leaders by their full names because we perceive them as more important than others, we tend to acknowledge support staff by first name only. Names make it possible for us to be seen and understood and to matter in the eyes of others. We may need to linger in conversation with someone in order to allow our connection to blossom. In that way, we see their name as a part of their whole being. Taking the time to learn and acknowledge people's full names means we can see them more fully, *l'olam*, in the world.

Rabbi Susan Leider is a part of the second cohort of the IJS Clergy Leadership Program and served as Senior Rabbi of Congregation Kol Shofar in Tiburon, CA.

She loves that Jonathan's heart guides his teaching, infusing care and compassion for all his students, who have been transformed by his deep Torah.

Vayelekh
Catching Glimpses Of A Hidden God

Aaron Schonbrun

A story is told about Rabbi Barukh of Medzhibizh, whose grandson Yehiel once came running into his study in tears. "Yehiel, why are you crying?" asked Rabbi Barukh. "My friend cheats! It's unfair; he left me all by myself!" "Would you like to tell me about it?" asked Rabbi Barukh. "Certainly Grandfather. We played hide-and-seek, and it was my turn to hide and his turn to look for me. But I hid so well that he couldn't find me. So he gave up; *he stopped looking.*" Tears welled up in Rabbi Barukh's eyes. "God too, Yehiel." he whispered softly," God too is unhappy; God is hiding and we, our people, are not even searching..." (adapted from Wiesel, *Four Hasidic Masters*, 52-53)

God is *nistar*, hidden, and humanity is not practiced at searching for, or even noticing the divine sparks that are all around. In *parashat Vayelekh*, as Moses's life comes to a close, we read that this hiding is intentional, a punishment for the children of Israel who will inevitably turn to false Gods after Moses's death (Deut. 31:18). The *Hiddushei Ha-Rim* explains God is so hidden, that people don't even realize that God is lacking in their lives (Greenberg, *Torah Gems*, 316.)

But as our story reminds us, God's presence need not remain hidden forever. Hidden among the poetry and song of our lives, hidden within our sacred texts, traditions, and human interactions, lies the presence and mystery that is the Holy One of Blessing – but only if we are willing to look. We say three times a day *karov Adonai l'kol kor'av.* (Ps. 145:18). God is close, but only if we are willing to call. Only, if we are willing to "turn in awareness" to the mystery that is hidden in all moments. With practice, persistence, and patience, we have the daily opportunity to recognize that the divine presence that we might have thought had abandoned us, or that we didn't even consider in the first place, has been here beside us all along.

And so, with love, compassion, and care, our Torah portion and our teacher, encourage each of us to sit in stillness and take time to notice.

Each day we are invited to sit quietly and ask: where is the sacred in my life, in my relationships, in this very moment? Each day we are taught to lift up that which seems ordinary, in recognition of the possibility that it might indeed be sacred and extraordinary. May we be blessed to be patient, mindful, and loving in this spiritual practice.

Rabbi Aaron Schonbrun is the spiritual leader of Congregation Torat El in Oakhurst, NJ.

He has been blessed to learn from Jonathan in the fourth cohort of the IJS Clergy Leadership Programand dedicates this teaching to him in gratitude for his kind heart, wise counsel, thoughtful demeanor, patience, and calming presence with all of his students.

Ha'azinu
Becoming Enough

Rex Perlmeter

In my work as a Spiritual Director, I have the blessing of "companioning" people in their inner journey with the Holy One. All too often, as they work toward that deeper conversation, I hear echoes of an inner dialog with themselves that goes something like this: "Oh, God. I have to do X. It's not going to be good enough…I'm not good enough…it's going to be lousy…I'm lousy…" – you get the drift. If we stayed on the train to the last station, I'm sure the signs at the stop would read, "It's going to be worthless," "I'm worthless.". Imposter syndrome is a common phenomenon in so many other life paths. Of course, there is good therapeutic work to be done in regard to such harsh self-judgment, but there is spiritual work as well.

Rabbi Moshe Chayyim Ephraim of Sudilkov, offers wonderful insight into how we might move to a different conversation with God, especially during the season of *teshuvah*. The rebbe takes as his inspiration Deuteronomy 32:10:

יִמְצָאֵהוּ בְּאֶרֶץ מִדְבָּר יִמְצָאֵהוּ בְּאֶרֶץ מִדְבָּר יִמְצָאֵהוּ בְּאֶרֶץ מִדְבָּר

[God] found him in a desert region,
In an empty howling waste.
[God] encircled him, watched over him,
Guarded him as the pupil of an eye.[*]

Rabbi Sam Feinsmith points out that the rebbe looks first at the verb *yevoneneihu* and reads it as an indication of God providing insight (a play on the word *binah)*. When insight is present, we are encircled by God – and to what might that refer? Within insight, we can allow ourselves to fall into the triangle of *chesed, gevurah and da'at/ emet*, where we can see things as they are and as they could yet be

---

[*] translation by Sam Feinsmith

from within a *sukkah* of accepting, unending love. Instead of saying "I cannot…" or "I am not…", this is the place from which we are able to say: "not yet." It is a place which moves us from imposing hateful labels upon ourselves and others to an aspiration and faith in our capacity to do and be better.

This suggests a spiritual practice within our spiritual practices. Whatever yours might be – prayer, meditation, study, yoga - notice when judging, comparing mind shows up – "I'm not doing it well enough; I can't do it well enough; I'm not good enough", and ask yourself, "Is this *binah?* Is this True understanding, originating in a field of Divine Love and Hope, or is it coming from a lower place?" Notice that these thoughts are just thoughts, and see if – upon recognizing that this is so – you can allow yourself to fall into the Love that inspires forgiveness and the courage to try again.

Rabbi Rex Perlmeter is a Special Advisor for Member Support and Counseling at the Central Conference of American Rabbis and a Spiritual Director to students at the Hebrew Union College-Jewish Institute of Religion.

He will be ever grateful to Jonathan for modeling the beats of silence that follow any question asked of him, during which it is clear he turns toward that field of Divine Love to discern the voice of Truth and respond from within that place.

Ve-zot Ha-berakhah
Eye See the End And It's the Beginning

David Schuck

The Torah ends with a declarative statement: there will never be another prophet of Moshe's stature. Moses was intimate with God; he saw God face to face. He was empowered to exhibit God's awesomeness לְעֵינֵי כָּל־יִשְׂרָאֵל, *before the eyes of all of Israel*.

Rabbi Baruch of Mezhibizh (1811) reminds us that when we complete the final verse of the Torah, we immediately read the first one: *In the beginning of God's creating heaven and earth...*When we tie the end and beginning of the Torah together, there is wisdom to be mined. He writes:

לפי עיני ישראל והסתכלותם בתורה, כך הוא חידוש מעשה ברא־
שית בכל יום.

As the people of Israel [use their eyes to] contemplate Torah, creation is renewed daily (Itturei Torah, *Ve-zot Ha-berakhah*)

The Torah ends by emphasizing the power of our eyes and minds to contemplate the world through the Torah. As we begin to read it again from the beginning, we immediately find ourselves in the story of creation. Reb Baruch suggests that this is not accidental. He reminds us that when our eyes are opened to the mysteries of the world and we use the Torah to approach those mysteries, something new emerges, a *chiddush*, and creation is renewed.

This is the power of mindfulness. If we live with our eyes open to what is actually happening, moment to moment, and we allow ourselves to bring our attention to the truth of our experience, something new emerges. It may be a feeling that was blocked, an embodied sensation from which we had detached, or perhaps even a repressed truth about our lives that suddenly comes into full focus. Each of these things- from the smallest bodily sensation to the deepest truth of our lives- is itself a *chiddush*, the emergence of something new (or perhaps something old that is new to us because we finally opened our eyes to it).

This *chiddush* joins the universe of God's creation. My new awareness of the truth of my life now takes its place among the expanse of the heavens and the bird that feeds its young. It is part of God's creation, and when I comprehend this, I understand that I too, am not separate from any living thing. I am part of that Creation.

The end of the Torah is also its beginning. The eyes of Israel lead us to creation which is ongoing and never ending. In our fortunate moments, we truly grasp this as we collapse into the unity of God's creating, alongside the mighty seas and wee little ant. If only we could stay in that knowing.

Rabbi David Schuck is a rabbi in New Rochelle, NY.
Rabbi Slater's voice is the voice he hears when he tries to quiet his mind and focus on the truth of my experience. It holds him in the vulnerability of that listening.

Modah Ani
Beginning with Gratefulness

Shefa Gold

מוֹדֶה אֲנִי לְפָנֶיךָ רוּח חַי וְקַיָּם שֶׁהֶחֱזַרְתָּ בִּי נִשְׁמָתִי בְּחֶמְלָה, רַבָּה
אֱמוּנָתֶךָ:

I gratefully acknowledge Your Face; Spirit lives and
endures;
You return my soul to me with compassion; How great
is your faith in me!

As human beings, we have inherited a brain from our stone-age
ancestors that is particularly alert to the possibilities of danger. Neu-
roscientists call this negativity bias. We are programmed to first notice
what's wrong. My prayer life is designed to overcome this negative
bias and open my heart to the blessing and miracle that God is giving me today.

Every spiritual tradition acknowledges that how we begin our day
matters. Each day I wake up with an intention that when I open my
eyes I will see and recognize God's face in the details of the day I am
about to encounter. If my very first expression is gratefulness (rather
than seeing what's wrong today or obsessing over how much I need
to get done) then I step on to a path of blessing. I prepare myself for
wonder.

With the first phrase of the prayer (*modah ani l'fanekha*), I open
to the miracle embedded in the day that is being given to me. For
the second phrase (*ruach chai v'kayyam*), I substitute *ruach* (Spirit)
for the traditional *melekh* (King). I acknowledge that although my
whole world is in flux, there is a Great Spirit — eternal and enduring,
moving through all of it.

With the third phrase (*shehechezarta bi nishmati b'chemla*), I become
receptive to the gift of consciousness from the Compassionate One
and I open to the sense of being seen, known, loved and fully accepted

by the Great Mystery that embraces me this very day.

The last phrase of the prayer (*raba emunatekha*) is taken from *Eikha,* the Book of Lamentations 3:23. When I experience God's faith in me, I receive a glimpse of the widest, longest perspective. In that glimpse, I am calmed. I relax my frantic grip. I stop trying to figure it out. I begin to trust the flow of inexorable change.

As God sees me, I surrender to that faithful gaze. This Divine faith in me is what grows my own fragile faith. When I am known, seen and loved completely through this Divine faith, I can dare to rise to the challenge of loving this world with all that I am and everything I've got.

Meister Eckart said that if the only prayer you ever say is, "Thank You," that would be enough.

Gratefulness connects us up to the great flow of receptivity and generosity. When we begin the day in gratefulness, we step on to the path of love.

Rabbi Shefa Gold leads workshops and retreats on the theory and art of chanting, devotional healing, spiritual community building and meditation.

Her beloved Jonathan, teacher and colleague, has helped her to ground herself in the sacred text. His gentleness and wisdom are an inspiration.

Elohai Neshamah
Gracious Recipient

Benjie Ellen Schiller

The soul, breath You have given me is pure.
You placed it within me, shaped it, breathed it into me;
You preserve it deep inside of me.

Our *neshamah* is the essence of life (*"tehorah hi."*) There is no separate "me" or "us" without it. It doesn't come *from* us. It is *placed* in us (*"atah y'tsarta."*) We are the recipient of this gift, bequeathed to us each moment we breathe in and out (*"atah n'fach'ta bi."*) We are kept alive by this gift. In each moment, we receive it anew (*"v'atah m'sham'ra b'kirbi."*)

The words of the prayer call to mind the poignant moment in the Torah when God breathes life into the clay human form:

> *And God formed humankind from the dust of the ground,*
> *And God breathed life into its nostrils, and the human became*
> *a living being. (Gen. 2:7)*

The following teaching from the *Sippurei Chasidim* addresses the underlying question inherent in this divine act:

> *Reb Yaakov Aryeh of Radzimin visited Menahem Mendel*
> *of Kotzk. The Kotzker immediately accosted him with this*
> *question: Why did the Holy One bother creating the human?*
> *Reb Yaakov responded that humans were created in order*
> *to elevate our neshamah, our soul-breath. The Kotzker*
> *countered that on the contrary, they both learned from their*
> *teacher, Simcha Bunem of Pshiskhe, that the Holy One*
> *created humans in order to elevate Heaven.*

As if to say, we were created to bring dignity to God's very self.

God imparts dignity by breathing breath into the human, and our act of acceptance – by breathing *ruach* back to God brings dignity back to its Source.

When we recite the words *"Elohai neshamah,"* we remind ourselves that this soul-breath has been given to us. We cannot breathe ourselves into being. The act of breathing is involuntary. Being animates us! It comes from God. To recognize this truth is to affirm the symbiotic connection between holiness and human existence. Each one of us is a vessel, a manifestation of God's presence through our very breath.

The task of a gracious recipient is to remember what has been given in each possible moment. (*"kol z'man shehaneshamah b'kirbi…"*) While we have the privilege of inhabiting this life, let us remember that our breath and soul are gifts to be accepted with appreciation. (*"modah ani l'fanekha."*) This is the way we bring honor back to the Source (*"ribon kol hamaasim, adon kol haneshamot."*)

How do we remember to remember? By being aware that we literally receive life. (*"asher b'yado nefesh kol chai."*) By inhaling and exhaling our thanks and praise. (*"v'ruach kol basar."*) This recognition that we are the beneficiaries of our breath may be the most profound expression of free will we humans can possibly offer.

Elohai neshamah – breathe in

Shenata bi – breath out

Tehorah hi – Pause. Feel the presence within.

Return the breath back to the Source of all Being.

Cantor Benjie Ellen Schiller is a professor at the Debbie Friedman School of Sacred Music of Hebrew Union College and serves as cantor of Bet Am Shalom Synagogue in White Plains, New York.

In word and deed, Jonathan teaches her what it means to live a life of mindfulness, as a friend, colleague, fellow davening partner, and sacred teacher.

Asher Yatzar
When I Sit and When I Go

Shmuel Birnham

This is the blessing said after using the toilet. But it is so much more than that.

A few points:

1. "What is the meaning of the *Echad* in the Shema? That there is no place empty of God." In other words, we can thank God at every moment in life. Every. Because God is present everywhere and at every moment.

2. In the 17th *berakhah* of the *amidah*: We thank You and praise You morning noon and night for Your miracles that attend us daily...

In other words, all day long, for everything, we can be thanking the Holy One.

3. Why do I thank God every time I get a parking spot? And now, living in a 25 ft RV, getting a parking spot is always a time to thank God for that miracle. I thank God for even though I know that God did not specifically help me to find that particular spot. It is a *nes*, a miracle. Every time. Just like going to the bathroom, breathing, walking, speaking, swallowing, standing, etc.

Specifically with *Asher Yatzar*, we are thanking God for the body working. Sadly, we often notice the body when it is not working. This *berakhah* sets out the brilliant idea of having gratitude for something actually working in a normal way. Remember, it didn't have to work. We know that there are people who cannot stand, walk, breathe with ease, or even use the bathroom.

As the *berakhah* says, "if one of the ducts was closed or couldn't open...." But it worked. Thank God. Be joyous.

Practice

All day long, when my body is working: standing, walking, biking, sitting, breathing, I take note. That is what this prayer taught me. It magnifies the so-called normal miracles that happen all the time—

the miracles we usually ignore or don't even think are miracles. When I do this, it magnifies my joy of the Present moment. And magnifies my sense of God's loving Presence, which really is always present.

I'm going to assume that you can remember each time after you go to the bathroom to thank God after it, when you're out of the bathroom. What about the rest of the day?

Set up a simple reminder system. Once an hour on the hour? When you look at the time on your watch or phone? Or during the day take 3, 5, 10, or more moments to consciously pause and take account of your gratitude vis a vis your body. You have your own medical-body history. Get in touch with it.

Just Celebrate.

You can change this, today.

You will smile.

God will smile.

Rabbi Shmuel Birnham is a retired rabbi who served in Asheville, NC and West Vancouver, BC and was a participant in the original cohort of the IJS Rabbinic Leadership Program.

He has known Jonathan since 1999 and has always been impressed, moved, and inspired by his dedication, integrity, intelligence, patience, as well as his ability and passion to teach.

Nissim B'khol Yom
The Miraculous Ordinary

Jason Rosenberg

The *nissim b'khol yom* are a series of blessings thanking God for daily miracles—opening the eyes of the blind, and clothing the naked. They aren't big, cinematic miracles, but rather the smaller, more prosaic miracles (as oxymoronic as that may be) which are so easy to miss.

But they are also seen as references to even smaller, more mundane acts—the acts involved with waking up in the morning. In this reading, "opening the eyes of the blind" is a reference to opening our own eyes after a night's sleep. "Clothing the naked," is getting dressed, and so on. Read this way, these blessings become a reminder of God's presence and of the potential for holiness in the most pedestrian of moments.

Of course, there are no pedestrian moments; there are just moments which are more obviously sacred, and those which better conceal the presence of the One than others. Everything—every single thing—contains some spark of holiness. Even the things which we routinely ignore (putting on clothes) or routinely loathe (the alarm waking us in the morning) have it.

So, it is according to the *Me'or Einayim* (*Likutim Shir Hashirim*). When he reads Proverbs 3:6, "Know God in all of your ways," he takes those words literally. In *all* of your ways. In everything that you do, you can know God. God is like a Ruler who dresses up to hide among Their people. A wise subject knows that the Ruler might be anywhere, and so is always careful to speak well of Them. Indeed, it's the case that God *is* anywhere, and everywhere, and we must constantly be aware of Their presence. But we don't do so for fear of offending or angering the Ruler, but because of how much joy it brings us to find God, wherever we may look.

What's truly wonderous is that, so often, the only trick to encountering something of holiness in these "lesser" moments is a willingness to see that holiness. When we put on our shoes, or brush our teeth, or stretch our arms, the simple decision to do so with a *kavvanah* of holiness is enough to make us aware of the holiness which has always been there. It takes nothing more than that to make any moment sacred. In everything that we do, we can know God.

Rabbi Jason Rosenberg is the rabbi of Congregation Beth Am in Tampa, FL and a participant in the first IJS Clergy Leadership Program.

He adores Rabbi Slater's gentle presence as a meditation leader, and the calm that he brings to the room.

Pesukei D'zimrah
God's House

George Gittleman

Ashrei yoshvei veitekha, od y'halelukhah selah/Happy are those who dwell in Your house; they forever praise You! (Psalm 84:5)

This verse is found at several points in our *siddur*, including *Pesukei D'zimrah/Verses of Praise* in the morning liturgy. What does it mean *to dwell in Your (God's) house?* How might this phrase from our liturgy inform our spiritual practice?

It could be that the Psalmist had an actual building in mind like the ancient Temple in Jerusalem. More likely, *Your house* is a metaphor for being in the Divine presence. The Hebrew word translated as "to dwell," *yosheiv,* can also mean to meditate. Perhaps *Your house* is not a physical location but a state of being. And if God is everywhere, every place could be *beitekha,* God's place.

If this is the case, it does not seem farfetched to suggest that learning to dwell in God's house — to live continually bathed in the Divine light — is the goal of spiritual practice. But life often seems anything but Divine. Suffering in various forms can define our daily lives, and moments of transcendence seem rare and fleeting. The challenge is to befriend the whole of our experience, to understand, as the Jewish mystical traditions teach us, *ein od milvado/There is no place devoid of the Divine.*

Ashrei yoshvei veitekha. Happy is the one who realizes that *this* place is Your place. The place I am in right now, with all the good and the bad, is God's place. *This* place, with all its suffering. *This* place, in all its glory. *This* place in my brokenness. *This* place in our pain. It is *all* God's place, and ours.

It's not, "when I get it right, I will be there." It's not "when I am happy, I will be there." We are in the Divine presence in the valley of the shadow, on the narrow bridge, in aversion, distraction, frustration, and restlessness. *Ein od milvado/There is no place that is not Your place.*

And when we realize that this is all God's place, *od y'halelukhah selah*, we praise You by being present, awake and alive right here, where You abide, which is within us.

Take a moment to settle. Feel into your body. Find your breath. And when you are ready, turn your awareness to whatever arises. Be like the sky, aware but unattached to the thoughts and feelings that arise, move through, and dissipate like the weather. Try not to push away or attach to anything. Rest in the awareness that it is all part of being in *beitekha/Your house/God's house.*

Rabbi George Gittleman and his spouse Laura were married by Rabbi Jonathan Slater in 1991. He has served as rabbi at Congregation Shomrei Torah since 1996. Since their first meeting, Jonathan has been his rabbi, mentor, colleague and friend.

Yotzer Or
Keeping the Life-Force Flowing

Suzanne Griffel

Me'or Einayim, Yitro 28

ונודע כי כל העולם עם כל הנבראים צריכים לקבל החיות מהבורא
ברוך הוא בכל עת ובכל רגע כמו שכתוב
ובטובו מחדש בכל יום תמיד מעשה בראשית כי במעשה בראשית
היה הבריאה על ידי חיות חדש שנאצל מהבורא ברוך הוא בכל
הנבראים וכמו כן גם בכל עת ובכל רגע צריכים שלא יופסק מהם
החיות תמיד ויושפע עליהם בתמידות ...

It is known that the whole world, including all created beings, must receive their life-force from the Blessed Creator at all times, moment by moment, as it is written, **"In God's goodness, God renews the work of creation continuously every day."** This is because during the creation of the world, creation happened by means of a new life-force that flowed from the Blessed Creator into all created beings; similarly, at all times and at every moment, they need for the life-force not to be stopped so it can flow into them continuously...

For many years it has been my practice to sit near a window during *Shacharit* and, when I come to *uv'tuvo m'chadesh b'khol yom tamid ma'aseh bereishit*, to turn my head, look out, and pay appreciative attention to the natural world. While this practice has long been a meaningful *kavanah* booster, it was only when I encountered this text that I realized I had been seeing the trees, grass, and whatever else was outside the window as separate from me. The *Me'or Einayim* opened my eyes (pun intended) to the fact that we are on the same team, connected every day and at every moment by the life-force flowing into us from the same Divine source.

This feels especially resonant - and urgent - as climate change accelerates and we increasingly feel its effects, including the extinction of up to 500 species in the last 100 years and the threat of the loss of over 500 more in the next 20 years. This cessation of the life-force from so many of our fellow earthmates isn't God's fault; it is a result of our failure to see the connection the *Me'or Einayim* describes so beautifully and to act accordingly. Now when I get to those words in *Yotzer Or*, I still look out the window and give thanks for the constant renewal of creation, and I also ask "What can I do, today, to help God keep us all going?"

Suzanne Griffel, a Reform-trained rabbi, has lived in Chicago for over 30 years and worked in Hillel, congregations, and chaplaincy. She is grateful to Jonathan for helping her see herself more clearly and in awe of his ability to do the same for so many people.

Ahavah Rabbah
Held in God's Love

Dan Liben

Why is this blessing, whose purpose is to acknowledge the gift of Torah, couched in the language of love? The answer seems clear: The act of Divine Revelation at Sinai is the ultimate expression of God's love for us.

The Hasidic tradition expands our understanding of Revelation itself. The *Netivot Shalom, Parashat Yitro*, reminds us that the unfolding Torah of our lives is as rich and as commanding as the voice first heard at Sinai:

> *"Listen to* My voice.*" Incline your hearts to hear what it is that God wants of you, to hear in everything the inner intention that is contained in the voice of God, what it is that God desires. This is the first element of being a Jew: to listen to the voice of God, to investigate in whatever comes your way: "what does God want of me?"; "what does YHVH your God ask of you" (cf. Deut. 10:12, Micah 6:8).*

Sometimes, the Torah unfolding before us is unpleasant, almost too difficult to bear. We don't really want to see our foibles and weaknesses, our missed opportunities, or the low spiritual level to which we have sunk. How can we survive that kind of self-scrutiny?

The blessing of *Ahavah Rabbah* reminds us that we can see and hold whatever Torah needs to be seen, because we are seen by the Holy One and held in God's loving embrace.

Practice:

Find a quiet place to practice, and allow your attention to focus on your breath. After a few minutes, direct your breath towards your heart. With each in-breath and out-breath, cultivate a felt sensation of energy emanating from your heart and gradually filling your body.

With each breath, sense that this energy is both emerging from within you, and from a greater source of Divine hesed, Loving Kindness. Feel yourself being held in a loving, Divine Embrace.

From this place of deep connection, offer the following prayer: "May God's loving embrace allow me to hold the truth." Allow yourself to reflect on one of the following questions: What does God require of me? What hidden thing is asking to be revealed?

Rabbi Dan Liben is Rabbi Emeritus of Temple Israel of Natick MA.. IJS transformed his priorities as a pulpit rabbi, and continues to deepen and inform his prayer life and mindfulness practice. One of the things he loves about Jonathan is the alacrity and joy with which he helps Hevraya find a text or a source!

Mi Kamokha
Silence in the Face of Awe

Ellen Lippmann

There has to be a better way to pray the *Mi Kamokha*. Every time, I think a gifted *Shaliach Tzibur* [prayer leader] will find a way to express the joy and wonder that must have filled the hearts of those freed Hebrew slaves. And every time, I feel let down. The song, the chant, just doesn't quite make it.

> *Who is like you, O God, among the gods that are worshiped?*
> *Who is like You, majestic in holiness, awesome in splendor,*
> *working wonders?*

Who is like You? The only right answer is "no one;" so how can humans possibly sing those words with adequate power? In 2022 or 5782, we need a new inspiration.

Levi Yitzhak of Berdichev, commenting in *Kedushat Levi* on the Torah portion *Ki Tavo*, offers us two possibilities.

First, as he wrote on Deuteronomy 26:17, "As a general rule the largesse dispensed by God ... is known as דבור, as we know from Psalms 33:6: בדבר ה' שמים נעשו וברוח פיו כל צבאם, "by the word of God the heavens were made and by the breath of God's mouth all their host." Whenever the Jewish people are on a spiritually lofty plateau, it is as if they cause God to dispense God's largesse for them.

Through words, God gives us power. Through words, we - aspiring to a "spiritually lofty plateau" - must answer: Maybe "poem" instead of "song"? "Then Moses and the Israelites spoke this poem to יהוה." Word reaching for word, דבור *to* שִׁירָה.

Second, in the same commentary Levi Yitzhak unknowingly offers a different possibility: If, God forbid, they (we) have fallen from that spiritual level, the Talmud (Gittin 56b) likens them to Exodus 15,11 מי כמוך באלם ה', which according to the Talmud should be read as מי כמוך באלמים, "who is like You amongst the silent ones?" [Reading אלם

as אלמים, silent ones]

Levi Yitzhak wants to disparage by seeing us as silent in a "can't speak" kind of way. But we discern something else here. If, as Levi Yitzhak reminded us, God created worlds through speech but also through רוח פיו – *ruach piv* - the breath of God's mouth, then we can reciprocate with silent breath as a means of praise. We can read, "*Who is like You among the silent?*", as "Who is like You, among the sitters in silence," Who is like You who creates through the act of breathing, and joins those who sit silently in the matching act of breathing?"

The best way to honor the power of that indescribable moment at the Sea is not to try to replace Moses and Miriam with song or words that will never suffice. Rather it is to sit in silence as we move from the Shema to the Amidah, a deep silence placed in us for just such a moment to match the breath from the mouth of our Creator.

Ellen Lippmann, part of the third cohort of the IJS Rabbinic Leadership Program is Rabbi Emerita of Kolot Chayeinu, a progressive congregation she founded in 1993. She learned from Jonathan Slater how to make small shifts that lead to big learning, how to sit in meditative silence, how to approach traditional prayer with respect and anticipation.

Amidah
Being God's Vessel

Mike Comins

Rabbi Chanina ben Dosa, known for the effectiveness of his prayers for healing, was asked how he knew that his prayer had been answered. He replied, "Whenever the prayer comes easily to my lips, I know that it has been accepted. When it does not, then I know that it has been rejected." (Berakhot 34b) One might have expected a different answer: the choice of words or the devotion of the heart. But we are never told why his prayer is answered. Rather, we learn that when his body and mind are attuned, when his attention is full and undistracted, he knows that his prayer aligns with Divine reality.

I am reminded of this teaching when approaching the Amidah. Three steps back, three steps forward, praying *sifatai tiftach*, "My God, open up my lips that my mouth tell your praises." This is an ultimate moment of *kavvanah* in Jewish practice, as the Amidah is the central prayer of Jewish liturgy. We are challenged to bring mental focus and purity of heart to our praying. Easier said than done.

Our efforts to gather *kavvanah* take one of two paths. Either we exercise our willpower, or we let it go.

In the first path, we might focus on the meaning of the introductory prayer, *sifatai tiftach*, to help us daven with full attention. We might visualize ancestors, personal or communal, to focus our *kavvanah* on the first prayer, the Avot. We might ask our hearts and minds, "What do I need to pray for today?"

The second path is the path of mindfulness. I focus attention on my body, particularly where my feet meet the earth. As I step backward and forward, I hear the sound of my saying *sifatai tiftach*, observing it wrap around my awareness. Then, before beginning to daven the Avot prayer, I might draw a deep breath and follow the sensations of air exiting my stomach and passing through my nostrils. Sometimes, I observe the breath many times before speaking.

There is no better way to leave the thinking mind than focusing on the senses, fusing mind to body. The purpose is to get out of my own way. In the words of the Maggid of Mezritch:

A person should be so absorbed in prayer that he is no longer aware of his own self. There is nothing for him but the flow of life: all his thoughts are with God...Nothing but God exists for you; you yourself have ceased to be.

As we make ourselves empty vessels for the Divine to fill, we notice that the Divine flows through us. When at our best, the Divine within addresses the Divine without. *Khiv'yakhol*, it is as if God is praying to God!

Rabbi Mike Comins is founder of the TorahTrek Institute for Jewish Wilderness Spirituality and author of A Wild Faith: Jewish Ways into Wilderness, Wilderness Ways into Judaism *and* Making Prayer Real: Leading Jewish Spiritual Voices on the Difficulty of Prayer and What To Do About It.

He has been friends with Jonathan for decades and has learned from him throughout. Jonathan have always gone the extra mile to support him in his spiritual journey and in his professional path, with patience, with knowledge, with understanding, and always, with a smile. He is grateful to his friend.

Prayer for Peace
Living Shalom

Alison Kur

שִׂים שָׁלוֹם טוֹבָה וּבְרָכָה חֵן וָחֶסֶד וְרַחֲמִים עָלֵינוּ וְעַל כָּל יִשְׂרָאֵל עַמֶּךָ

One might think that eighteen benedictions are enough.

Yet without the nineteenth blessing of the Amidah, (grant peace...) we would be without *shalom*, the plea that would make us whole if answered.

Binyamin ben Aharon of Zalocze explains what it takes to be redeemed from our enemies in his commentary on *parashat Beha'alotekha* in *Torei Zahav* (pub. 1816).

Likening the enemy to the evil inclination, he teaches that we must first struggle with the enemy inside - with our own character traits and evil desires.

We must be redeemed ourselves, he says, before we can seek redemption for the community.*

Birkat Shalom contains within its words our pathway to *shalom* - to redemption and wholeness.

The opening guides us to open our hearts and shape our souls with טוֹבָה (goodness), בְּרָכָה (blessing), חֵן (grace), חֶסֶד (lovingkindness), and רַחֲמִים (mercy). This is the pursuit of our lives.

Meditate on each of these words.

Ask yourself where is this goodness, blessing, grace, lovingkindness, and mercy in my life?

Imagine yourself increasing in each of these pathways to shalom.

Conclude your practice:

בָּרְכֵנוּ אָבִינוּ כֻּלָּנוּ כְּאֶחָד בְּאוֹר פָּנֶיךָ

God, bless all of us as one in the light of Your Presence. Perhaps,

---

* Binyamin ben Aharon of Zalocze, *Torei Zahav*, translated in Speaking Torah, vol. 2, Arthur Green, [Woodstock, Vermont: Jewish Lights Publishing, 2013], pp. 19-20.

today, in this fleeting moment, just as I recite these words, I am re-deemed, connected to the One by whose light, we are all redeemed and made whole.

בָּרוּךְ אַתָּה ה' עושה השָׁלוֹם

Blessed are you, *Adonai*, the One who inspires us with the vision of *shalom*.

Alison Kur is a teacher and lover of Torah, who seeks to walk a path toward shalom and inspire others to find their own paths. She is deeply grateful to Jonathan for guiding her during the most difficult time in her life and for reminding her often that there is no bottom to the well of love.

The Kaddish
The Light of Torah

Suzanne Singer

What became known as thee Mourner's Kaddish began as a prayer to conclude Torah study. Torah study has, of course, been an integral part of IJS. Beginning with an introduction during my IJS Rabbinic Cohort 12 years ago, we have been guided through powerful Hasidic texts. My *hevruta* partner, Eric Rosin, and I have been inspired by studying these texts ever since. I want to comment on Jonathan Slater's summary of a *derash* on *Bereshit* by Rabbi Menahem Nahum of Chernobyl encapsulates the deep benefits of *Torah lishmah* – Torah study for its own sake:

> Dedicated Torah study prepares us to become righteous. Through it we make Torah our own, finding our place in the divine flow. The light present in Torah will turn us toward the good. Basking in the divine light, we are more able to rectify our past deeds...making them whole...As our past becomes whole, we are made whole as well. Our wholeness is constituted of both darkness and light, our flawed past and conscious present...R. Nahum reads the phrase "God said 'Let there be light', and there was light" as a response to our dedicated practice, our deep desire to become whole...R. Nahum assures us: there is light already.

This beautiful summary explains how meditation can be a means of developing mindfulness, freeing us from the grip of our past. Suffering is our response to pain. Through mindfulness, we can avoid personalizing the pain, thereby reducing how much pain we experience. Mindfulness allows us to observe our recurring negative thoughts without giving them the fuel to dictate our actions. This enables us to heal from past wounds. In addition, we can be more effective in our interactions with others. Rather than be driven by anger or sorrow or self-righteousness, we can thoughtfully consider how we wish to respond to a person or a situation. Mindfulness can separate our judgement from the reality outside of us, connecting us to the divine flow of goodness, unity, and light underlying it all.

Practice:

Try using the words of the Kaddish as a meditation. The repeated *hitpalel* pattern of the verbs (yit*gadal,* v'yit*kadash,* yit*barakh,* v'yisht*abakh,* etc.) has a hypnotic quality that can help you reach a meditative state. As you recite the words, think of light surrounding you and keeping you warm and safe.

Suzanne Singer has been the rabbi at Temple Beth El in Riverside, CA for 14 years. Prior to becoming a rabbi, she was a television producer, earning two national Emmys. She is so grateful to Jonathan for his compassionate teaching that allowed her to open up to these texts.

Hallel
Grounding Joy in Equanimity

Heather Batchelor

The mitzvah of Shabbat is the bliss (oneg) which is in one's mind — absent excitement or embodied devotion. Therefore, Shabbat doesn't encompass Hallel or gaiety (simcha). But the mitzvah of Yom Tov is in Hallel, gaiety and embodied devotion. Simcha spreads right out to one's extremities, until it sometimes brings one to the point of dancing....

Though it is good to serve Hashem with excitement and embodied devotion... it should come from a place of equanimity (yeshuv ha-da'at)...Without equanimity in one's rejoicing, what results? Though one imagines in their soul that such passion and devotion is the way of Hashem, it is but a mere fantasy.

Shem MiShmuel, *Vayigash* 7:11 & *Terumah* 2:11

According to the Shem MiShmuel (Rabbi Samuel Bornsztajn c.1910 - c.1926), Hallel is about exuberant joy (even to the point of dancing!), and yet that exuberance should be grounded equanimity. I love this idea, because I always look forward to letting loose during Hallel. But I also recognize that my thirst for ebullience can sometimes become a kind of striving — as if the "high" of devotion was something to be attained. Then *pursuing* joy becomes a fantasy — just like chasing an achievement or possession — a distraction from the lived experience of true joy.

Practice:

Before beginning, I invite you to find a line from Hallel that stirs joy. If you do not have a favorite line, try this one:

זֶה־הַיּוֹם עָשָׂה יְהוָה נָגִילָה וְנִשְׂמְחָה בוֹ:

This is the day that the Lord has made—

Let us exult and rejoice in it. (Psalms 118:24)

Come to a comfortable position: upright, yet at ease, eyes closed or gaze lowered.

Begin by observing your breath with open attentiveness.

If your mind wanders, just take note of this and bring your attention back to your breath.

Continue this way until your mind has settled and your thoughts are quiet.

Once your mind has settled, turn to your line from Hallel. Give it your full attention — perhaps reading it aloud or singing to yourself.

Now turn your attention inward and notice what images, memories or emotions arise for you. Explore with curiosity — just noticing what is there. You may wish to repeat your line, noticing any changes or shifts as you do so.

Once you have given yourself an opportunity to explore your inner experience of this bit of Hallel, return your attention to the anchor of your breath — allowing yourself whatever time you need for your thoughts to settle into quiet equanimity.

Cantor Heather Batchelor lives in Montreal, where she is a freelance cantor/educator, the spiritual leader of the Ruelle Shul and recently completed a thesis on Hasidic dance as an embodied spiritual practice.

According to the midrash, each infant is created intuiting the whole of Torah, but upon birth an angel strikes them upon the lips — initiating them to the world of speech and causing them to forget their inborn sacred knowledge. Learning with R' Slater hints that this sacred intuition might live in concert with the spoken and written word.

Yedid Nefesh
Love-Sickness

Les Bronstein

Central to Rabbi Elazar Azikri's radically sensual liturgical poem *Yedid Nefesh* is the image of love-sickness. The poem presents a brokenness that must be healed, elsewise the *paytan* (the liturgical poet) cannot go on, either with prayer or with life.

The *paytan* refers to one of the most painful moments in the Torah, that of Miriam's leprosy and Moses's spontaneous prayer for her recovery. Why else would the *paytan* do so except to compare his own striving for divine closeness to that of Moses transcending his insult to achieve healing for his beloved sister?

Moses is already *ne'eman beito*, the soul closest to God's inner self. Yet, he cannot access his own closeness until the person who saved him from death as an infant finds her own path back to wholeness. Moses knows that her physical ailment is a manifestation of her spiritual illness. He knows this is why she insults him so deeply, and why she must be healed before she can mend her relationship with him.

In this sense, the break between Miriam and Moses parallels the break we all experience between ourselves and the Holy One. We long to befriend our Soul Mate, our *yedid nefesh*, the source of our own true meaning. Why is it so hard to make the leap from the proficient articulation of our prayers to the point of feeling close to our Beloved? Partly because we are broken off from those we love, including our own essential self-love.

Rebbe Nachman, in his Likutei Moharan (105:4:1) meditates on the verse in Numbers 12:13 (*eil na r'fa na la* – "Please, God, please heal her") that sits in the middle of *Yedid Nefesh*. He asks why the word *na* is repeated in this short prayer. He tells us that he "heard" it explained that Moses asked this of God: that God, as it were, should pray and petition God's own self to heal her. In other words, Moses said to God, 'O God, I pray (*na*) that You Yourself pray (*na*) - *to* Yourself.'"

As we recite the *Yedid Nefesh* upon entering the shadows of Shabbat eve, and then again as the shadows darken at Shabbat's end, we might keep in mind our own disconnect from our best self – from the Divine *yedid* that lives in all of us. On Friday we allow ourselves to experience the hurt we carry with us into Shabbat, and at *se'udah sh'lisheet* we let ourselves be in touch with the pain that a restful Shabbat has not fully resolved. We think of those we have hurt and those who have hurt us.

In response, we recite Moses's bold prayer, *eil na r'fa na la*, and allow our soul to close the gap between itself and the Self who longs to love us. We implore our *Yedid* to *pray to itself on our behalf.* We should not put off our supplication. *Ki va mo'ed*, says the *paytan*. "The time is now."

Rabbi Azikri envisions that closing this gap of pain and unforgiveness would be *minofet tzuf v'khol ta'am*, sweeter than honey from the comb, the source of sweetness itself.

Les Bronstein is the rabbi of Bet Am Shalom Synagogue in White Plains. He has the privilege of davening with Jonathan on Shabbatot over the course of many years, and of learning both the Torah of texts and of patience directly from Jonathan.

L'kha Dodi
Creating Real Welcome

Evan Kent

In my 30 plus years as a congregational cantor, I have led numerous Kabbalat Shabbat services. I love how the liturgy of psalms and songs leads us with a slow and gradual reveal to the moment of welcoming Shabbat into our midst with the singing of *L'kha dodi*. Within *L'kha dodi*, there is an increasing anticipation of welcoming the Sabbath Bride with the culminating text: "*Bo-i khallah, bo-i khallah.*"

Rabbi Schneur Zalman of Liadi taught that on Shabbat, the masculine force of God, the Beloved, descends and lifts the feminine energy of the Bride back to the upper spiritual realms. Thereby, it infuses or inseminates the "Kallah" with a renewed radiance. We rejoice and celebrate this metaphorical sexual union while singing, "*L'kha dodi likrat kallah.*" With the singing of the last lines of *L'kha dodi*, we turn to the main entrance of the synagogue and bow to greet this bride. This moment of welcoming and celebrating the Shabbat is so entrenched in our liturgy (and in our hearts, souls, and singing voices) that only recently have I realized that *L'kha dodi* celebrates a moment of heterosexual marriage and sexual union (albeit metaphorical).

Even as metaphor (and like all prayer, *L'kha dodi* is metaphor), I question the semantic implications of this piyyut and the appropriateness of wedding and sexual imagery as a gateway into Shabbat. As a gay man, I am excluded from this heteronormative sexual imagery, and until recently I was also excluded from the legal rite of marriage. Additionally, *L'kha dodi* presents issues of power and hierarchy, not something I want to be part of my observance of Shabbat. Just as liberal Judaism has adapted other prayers to reconcile changing concepts of sexuality, relationships, and gender equality, I propose an examination of this cherished text.

In Israel, Rabbi Efrat Rotem proposed replacing *L'kha dodi* with the "*Al ahavatekha*" by Yehudah HaLevi (Ben-Lulu, 2019) and the new Israeli Reform Movement's siddur "Tefillat Ha-Adam" includes

"*Al Ahavatekha*" as an alternate text to *L'kha dodi*. The seven verses of the poem, present a worker "raising his cup" to the Seventh Day. Rather than a hierarchical relationship, Halevi presents a relationship of mutuality. The opening stanza states:

> To you I raise my cup:
> Shalom, peace to you, my Seventh Day.
> The six workdays enslaved to you,
>   even though I work, I wander aimlessly.
> They seem to me to blur into one,
>   because of my love for you, day of enjoyment.

The singing of *L'kha dodi* is one of the most treasured moments of our Friday night worship. But perhaps the time has come to replace *L'kha dodi* itself with a poem of love based on equality and mutuality.

Cantor Evan Kent served Temple Isaiah in Los Angeles as its senior cantor for 25 years. He currently lives in Jerusalem and teaches at HUC-JIR.

He thanks Jonathan, for opening his eyes to wonder and opening my soul to the infinite nature of the Almighty.

Ma'ariv Aravim
Discovering the Creator in the Darkness

Rachel Goldenberg

The *ma'ariv aravim* blessing praises the Holy One who rolls light away from darkness and darkness from light, bringing the evening.

It can be difficult to accept that day turns to night. Society expects us to be in constant motion, always productive, and it can feel wrong to rest and allow night to come. Like Shabbat, every evening requires us to let go of what is undone.

I resist the evening, perhaps because when it gets dark and quiet, I must be with myself more intimately. At night it is harder to distract myself from the worries and obsessions of my mind. Work is done. The dishes have been washed. And now all there is, is this heart and this mind. I'd rather scroll on my phone than be with myself, here, in the dark.

How do I live these words: Praised are You who brings on the evening? How do I find Divinity in the dark?

Rebbe Nahman teaches that we can experience the Divine presence within the very obstacles that obscure God from view. We can find expansiveness within constriction; big mind within little mind.

When the Israelites stand at Mount Sinai, a thick cloud covers the mountain. Exodus 20:18 reads: "So the people remained at a distance, while Moses approached the thick cloud where God was."

God hides in the cloud, according to the Rebbe. He writes: "Thus, someone with awareness will look at the obstacle and discover the Creator there. "

Moses, who corresponds to the Israelites' collective quality of *da'at*, or awareness, is able to enter the cloud and see God's presence clearly.

As I bless the evening, I invite myself into the dark cloud in order to investigate it with curiosity. As I come close to the fear, the restlessness, or whatever blocks me from welcoming the night — I see my own suffering. With awareness, I can name the suffering and bring myself compassion. I find love – perhaps even God — in the dark.

Practice:

As evening comes and you finish your work, set aside a few minutes to sit in stillness. Find a relaxed yet alert position, close your eyes, bringing awareness to the breath. Pay attention to your state of mind and heart. What thoughts, feelings, or sensations are most prominent? Without analyzing or judging, sit in loving awareness with whatever "clouds" arise within you. Soften and open around any constriction. Close your practice with the words, *"Barukh Atah Yah, ha-ma'ariv aravim,"* "Praised are You, Creator, who makes evening— evening." See what happens. Does your relationship to the evening change?

Rabbi Rachel Goldenberg is the founder of Malkhut: progressive Jewish spirituality in Queens and an alumna of the IJS Rabbinic Leadership and Jewish Mindfulness Meditation Teacher Training programs.

What she most loves and appreciates about her teacher, Rabbi Jonathan Slater, is his deep compassion and humble guidance to always check his teachings against our own experience.

Ahavat Olam
Channeling God's Eternal Love

Scott Buckner

A carpenter was having a tough day. First, he had a flat tire that cost him an hour of work, then his electric saw quit, and finally his pickup truck refused to start. When he arrived home at the end of the day, he paused briefly at a small tree, touching the tips of the branches with both hands. Then he entered the house with big smiles and hugs for his children and a kiss for his wife. When asked about his ritual of touching the tree, he would say: "That's my trouble tree. I just hang up my troubles on the tree every night when I come home. They don't belong in the house with my wife and children."

This story illustrates that love requires us to be fully present. If our heads are filled with complaints about the past or worries about the future, how can we truly love? The actions of the carpenter reveal one of the greatest secrets of a meaningful life. How we show up in a relationship is dependent on setting an intention and maintaining a practice. It's too easy to get caught up in our problems and forget how this affects us and those around us. Acknowledging that we are part of something much greater than we realize can be an antidote for self-centered rumination.

The Hasidic masters understand the Shema as a reminder to dwell in *Echad* ("one"), at one with God and with all creation. Each evening, after reciting *Ahavat Olam*, linger in silence before the Shema. During the silence, focus your mind and heart on a time when you felt loved, perhaps by a past act of caring. Be like the carpenter. Take a moment to release your troubles and contemplate with gratitude how the love you have received allows you to turn outward with love. Let go of what you may perceive as deficient in your life and turn your heart fully to those you profess to love. Allow the energy of that love to flow through you and then to surface during the recitation of the Shema. Fully inhabit the first paragraph of the Shema, Ve-ahavta - to love God with all your heart, with all your soul and with all your might. These are the building blocks of a righteous life.

Cantor Scott Buckner, a participant in the first cohort of the Institute's Cantorial Leadership Program, leads Israel Congregation in Manchester, VT.

Jonathan's friendship, guidance and teaching has been at the center of his experience with the Institute. Sharing a kayak with Jonathan in Alaska during an IJS retreat is one of the highlights of their many years of friendship.

Mah Tovu
Sanctifying the Imperfect and Perfecting the Profane

Lisa D. Grant

The opening line of the prophet Balaam's blessing in Numbers 24:5, מה טובו אוהלך יעקב משכנתך ישראל, invites us to consider how we might turn curses into blessing in our lives. That is sufficient in and of itself, but when the verse is repurposed as liturgy to help us build sacred intention for entering a space of prayer, the layers of interpretation grow even richer with potential. These six words contain two doublets. What are we to make of the distinctions between a tent and a sanctuary, and the two different names of our third Patriarch, Jacob and Israel?

The *Degel Machaneh Ephraim* (Balak 14) reminds us that a tent is a temporary space in contrast to the *Mishkan*, which he describes as permanent and fixed. He suggests that we move from this private personal space to the communal space of the *Mishkan,* through "the merit of our ancestors" in order to draw closer to God. Along similar lines, the *Ohev Yisrael* (Balak 1:1) interprets the verse as saying the transition from Jacob to Israel moves us from an absence of Godliness, to one of *devekut*, unity with the Divine.

Together, these two commentators suggest that we move from the personal to the collective, from the material to the sacred. Jacob, the individual, moves from his temporal space of home to become Yisrael, the collective, who gather together in the sanctuary that the entire community of Israel built, to feel God's presence. Associating the tent with our far from perfect patriarch, Jacob, connects the transitory with our human limitations and flaws. Connecting the more spiritually elevated Yisrael, to the *Mishkan* can be seen as an invitation to move from a space of imperfection to one of sanctity and perfection.

Another reading of the verse upends the binary distinction between home and sanctuary. Rather than a move from one place and one identity to another, perhaps we can see this as a "both/and." Yisrael is both the individual and the collective. We must bring our full selves into the *Mishkan* in order for it to be truly holy. While we might read *ohel* as a modest, private dwelling, the word is also used as a dwelling place for God. The *ohel* is far from devoid of God. As the *Ohev Yisrael* suggests, sometimes we need the temporal and material to build our awareness of God's presence.

When we see that Jacob, in all of his imperfections, can draw close to God, so too, can we. This realization might take place while we are in the *Mishkan,* but the practice must take place in our tents, the places where we live, work, and love. The *Mishkan* is the idealized place of holiness, but it is in the actual daily spaces of our tents where we must work to bring God in.

Rabbi Lisa D. Grant, Ph.D. is the Eleanor Sinsheimer Distinguished Service Professor in Jewish Education and Director of the NY Rabbinical Program at HUC-JIR.

She is filled with gratitude to Jonathan, the teacher who opened her heart to God in more ways that she can number.

Kol Haneshamah
Breathing Practice for
Cultivating *Hitlahavut*/Enthusiasm

Lizzie Shammash

R. Levi Yitzchak of Berdichev, *Kedushat Levi*, Rosh Hashana

We must always try to bring to our consciousness that from moment to moment the Blessed Creator, in great love and mercy, instills in us a new vital force (*chiyut chadash*); from moment to moment the Blessed Creator renews our very being. This is what the rabbis meant when they said (regarding Psalm 150:6): **"for each and every breath praise Ya"H"** (Genesis Rabbah 14:10). That is, at each moment the breath seeks to leave us. The Blessed Holy One, in great mercy, watches over us from moment to moment and has compassion on us. God does not let the breath depart. In this manner, when we raise this thought to awareness, from moment to moment we actually are created anew as a new creature. This generates enthusiasm (*hitlahavut*) to serve the Blessed Creator, since everything that is new or renewed ignites enthusiasm. Since we are created anew from moment to moment, we can burn with that same enthusiasm in the service of the Holy Creator.

We can engage in a simple breath practice to experience or renew "basic enthusiasm," *hitlahavut*, by connecting with the pause between exhale and inhale.

Find a comfortable seat, distributing weight evenly through your feet on the floor and your sitting bones (base of your pelvis) in the chair. Allow the eyes to close, or keep your gaze soft. Relax your eyelids, brow and temples. Let your spine lengthen in two directions, upward and downward, creating space in your lower back, torso, throat and neck.

Bring your awareness to your breath, coming and going. Feel the abdomen and ribcage expanding on the in-breath and contracting on the out-breath. In and out. Follow this for several breath cycles, becoming interested in nuance- the texture of the breath, temperature, rate at which it moves. You do not need to change anything or apply effort. Simply notice any sensations that may arise.

You might begin to notice that at the end of the exhalation, there is a space- a stillness- before the inhalation returns. Can you feel that moment of "nothing" happening? For the next several breath cycles, bring your attention to that spacious pause. Anchor your attention there. Notice the vulnerability of that suspension where your life-force (*chiyut*) is held in the balance. It is true that the next in-breath is not guaranteed. It is the gift of the Divine Source. Notice how fresh, how welcome the next inhale is. Feel the sense of renewal and *hitlahavut*/enthusiasm for your own consciousness that accompanies the in-breath.

You can explore this practice in many positions. It can be especially nice in child pose or in constructive rest position (lying supine with knees bent, soles of feet on the floor, elbows bent and hands resting on your belly, palms facing down).

When I take a moment now and then throughout the day to notice my breath in this way, I am able to cultivate appreciation for Divine generosity and love, *chesed*.

Cantor Lizzie Shammash serves Adath Israel in Merion Station, PA, participated in the first cohort of the IJS Clergy Leadership Program and in the IJS Jewish Mindfulness Meditation Teacher Training program. She serves on the faculty of the CLP and teaches the IJS weekly Online Yoga Studio which grounds Talmud Torah in embodied practice.

She appreciates Jonathan's wisdom, wit, compassion and steadiness. This text was the very first one she studied with Jonathan.

Tefilat HaDerekh
I Shall not Fear, for You are Near

Lisa Bellows

Selections from Reb Nosen's Traveler's Prayer*:

O God and God of our fathers and mothers, have compassion on me and be with me at all times—when I sit in my house or go out on a journey, when I lie down and when I rise up, when I go out and when I come in, always give me true guidance as to what I should do regarding travel. Help me know whether to travel or not, how and when to travel, where to, which places I should include in my route, how long I should stay away, and all the details of the actual journeys—should I take the main road or a minor road, the long route or a shorter route. Loving God, guide me in everything and lead me along the [right] path, always.

Grant me grace, compassion and lovingkindness in Your eyes and in the eyes of all who see me.

Deal with me tenderly and bring me home in peace, whole in my body and soul....

Have compassion on me and be with me at all times: I pause, resting my body and mind from going and doing, and receive your compassion and love in quiet awareness. On the in-breath, I breathe in compassion; on the out-breath, I return compassion back into the world, only to receive again and again, each moment by moment.

When I sit in my house or go out on a journey: I do not need to travel or set out on an adventure to want You with me. I need Your love and gentle embrace wherever I am, wherever I go. God, help me feel your presence in my life's journey, that I may take shelter in your Divine embrace.

Help me know whether to travel or not. Help me know whether I am moving towards love, compassion, and kindness, for this is the

---

* *The Fiftieth Gate Likutey Tefilot Reb Noson's Prayers. Vol 2*, Trans. By Avraham Greenbaum. [Jerusalem/New York: Breslov Research Institute, 1993] p. 661, 663. Edited trans. by author.

road I want to travel.

Deal with me tenderly and bring me home in peace, whole in my body and soul: Breathing in I feel my body on the chair, my feet touching the floor, feeling the power Mother Earth. The crown of my head reaches towards the heavens. I sit between heaven and earth feeling Your power and grace. I am whole. I shall not fear, for You are near.

Rabbi Lisa Sari Bellows is the Senior Rabbi of Congregation Beth Am in Buffalo Grove, IL.

Jonathan's passion and skill for teaching, translating, and interpreting texts has brought her much joy and connection. She is forever grateful.

Tu Bishvat
Songs of Grasses, Trees, Creation

Robin Damsky

עָנָה רַבֵּנוּ ז"ל וְאָמַר: "אִם הָיִיתָ זוֹכֶה לִשְׁמֹעַ אֶת קוֹל הַשִּׁירוֹת
וְהַתִּשְׁבָּחוֹת שֶׁל הָעֲשָׂבִים, אֵיךְ כָּל עֵשֶׂב וְעֵשֶׂב אוֹמֵר שִׁירָה לְהַשֵּׁם
יִתְבָּרַךְ, בְּלִי פְּנִיָה וּבְלִי שׁוּם מַחֲשָׁבוֹת זָרוֹת וְאֵינָם מְצַפִּים לְשׁוּם
תַּשְׁלוּם גְּמוּל, כַּמָּה יָפֶה וְנָאֶה כְּשֶׁשּׁוֹמְעִין הַשִּׁירָה שֶׁלָּהֶם וְטוֹב מְאֹד
בֵּינֵיהֶם לַעֲבֹד אֶת ה' בְּיִרְאָה".

The Rebbe [Nahman] spoke: "If only you could be
privileged to hear the songs and the praises of the
grasses, how each and every blade of grass sings out
its song to the Blessed Creator, without any distracting
thoughts and without expectation of any reward. How
good and lovely it is when you hear their song. And it
is very good when among them to worship the Holy
Blessed Creator with reverence."
—*Sichot HaRan* 163.3, Rebbe Nahman of Bratzlav

What is the song of a blade of grass? Note how this blade holds
you in its arms, how it offers its teaching to you. Listen. Touch if it
helps, stroke. Be One. And receive.

Each and every blade of grass has its own song. So does each leaf
of a tree, each trunk, each root system. If we listen closely, without
distraction (*machshevot zarot*), if we become present with the soil-
being within – the *adam*/human created from the *adamah*/soil – we
can not only hear the song of each individual blade of grass, we can
hear the harmonies of the grasses. We can then tune our attention
to distinguish these melodies from the songs of each tree leaf, trunk
and root. For the sound of a trunk is very different from the song
of its leaf, and its roots sing a different melody entirely. Yet heard
altogether, we can even feel in our bones the chorus that each tree
composes. What richness, then, the symphony of a grove or forest

with all its trees, shrubs, herbs and grasses. How can we hear? How can we smell? How can we feel? It begins with creating a relationship with one blade of grass, one leaf, one trunk. In time, we can hear the symphony of the green world whose exhale is our very inhale.

The privilege of which Rebbe Nahman speaks is the gift of presence. How precious the space is when we are truly engaged, and connected. What we can hear, see, feel, taste and touch when we are connected to Sacred Spirit is a true privilege. That sense of connection is prayer itself.

Tu Bishvat is one calendar reminder for us to take time to listen, notice, and feel. Ideally, we can bring this into our lives regularly, yet on Tu Bishvat, we make a specific intention to invest in this connection.

Practice:

Go outside and find grass, a tree, or a shrub. If being outside is completely impossible, find an indoor plant. Or watch a beautiful nature video of grasses and trees. Settle. Breathe. Feel your soil-self, your *adamah*-ness. Then listen. Touch, if possible, even smell the *esev* – the green – that Spirit has put forth. You might notice synesthesia. Smell its beauty. Feel and hear its song. Sense your part of the song, how you are an integral voice of this symphony, this dance of creation. Feel your wholeness as intertwined with the wholeness of All. Listen to its teaching. Take it in. Let it sit. Then bring forward what is yours to share to help bring forth the songs of the green things to others and help heal the future for this majestic symphony.

Rabbi Robin Damsky leads Limitless Judaism, working with the interconnectedness of Body-Spirit-Gaia for personal and planetary well-being.
Jonathan's careful attention, kindness and selfless honesty continue to guide and inspire her.

Purim
The Ultimate Masquerade

Shira Milgrom

It is written: "Know God in all your ways." (Proverbs 3:6) All your deeds should be for the sake of heaven, even when you are engaged in worldly matters. Everything that exists is "the work of God for God's own sake." (Proverbs 6:140 The glory of God is present in each thing.

Regarding a king of flesh and blood, the king and his glory are not the same. But in God's case, it is all one, as the enlightened will understand. Thus, everything contains the glory of God; "the whole earth is filled with God's Presence." (Isaiah 6:3) There is no place devoid of God. Everything a person does of worldly things, eating and drinking, as well as business matters, is all God's presence.

Here is a parable: A king of flesh and blood disguised himself in varied garments. He would regularly go out among his troops that way, unrecognized by them. He wanted to see and hear what was going on among them. The clever ones, knowing the king's ways, were constantly aware lest the king be in their company in one of his guises. They were careful not to say anything improper."

The same is true (despite the vast differences) of the exalted One. God, too, is dressed in many guises. The Torah says, 'I indeed will hide My face – *hasteir astir.*' (Deuteronomy 31:18) This refers to costumes and hidings; God is always there, in costumes and disguises.
—*Me'or Einayim* (Rabbi Menahem Nahum of Chernobyl)

This text highlights three religious impulses central to my Jewish practice:

- All of life is sacred (God masquerades as everything)

- Joy is deeper than sorrow (costumes, masquerades, let your hair down, laugh)

- Act in this world for justice (In a time of God's hiddenness – a time of *hesteir* - be Esther – be the one who acts.)

- Practice related to joy and wonder: Saying berakhot for lightning, thunder and rainbows

Alternatively, reflect or meditate on this "Hasidic haiku":

Purim masquerade
God's hidden in everything
Take off masks and see

Rabbi Shira Milgrom is lucky to be learning about love with Congregation Kol Ami in White Plains NY, where she has been rabbi for 36 years.
IJS introduced her to a world of Hasidic texts and wisdom; these changed the 'what' and the 'why' that she studied, and in turn changed her rabbinate. Jonathan made possible this sea change for me and for so many others.

Pesach
Going Out of Egypt
A Continuous Spiritual Practice

Lauren Tuchman

On seder night, we embark on a holy commemorative journey through the Haggadah as we move spiritually and temporally from degradation to praise. We do not merely recount by rote our journey out of *Mitzrayim*, out of the narrowness to a wide expanse, but we engage in holy reenactment of the experience.

In Mishnah *Pesahim* 10:5, it is taught that in every generation, every single one of us is obligated to see ourselves as though we, too, went out of Egypt. We aren't only recounting the origin story of our ancestors, passed down generation after generation. We are part of the holy collectivity. We are active participants, not passive observers.

The Telling that we ritually experience on Pesach is not only about remembering our people's foundational story. Indeed, this story is so central that we are asked to recall it every day of our lives. Rather, Pesach is such a momentous event in spiritual terms that it is our duty to be actively shaping that experience for ourselves in every generation.

We move from the narrow place to one of wide expanse, a place devoid of God consciousness to one suffused with it. We move from a sense of degradation to praise, of owning our own narrative, no longer allowing others to define or shape it for us. We think about what represents *Mitzrayim* in our own lives. What are those things from which we cannot seem to free ourselves? Can we find liberation and possibility after years of being weighed down by our story and by our fear.

In every generation, we are each obligated to perceive ourselves as if we, too, left Egypt. The promises God makes to our ancestors, which we recount on seder night apply to us as much as they did to those who came before. Our physical and social locations in the great arc of the universe as a people have undergone tremendously radical shifts over the generations and yet, we return, again and again, to this fundamental theological truth. We, too, were there, a part of the story, obligated to bring its power into our lives. Maybe we choose one thing this Pesach we yearn to break free from. Maybe we set modest goals for ourselves. My anxiety might not vanish overnight, perhaps, or perhaps this one gnarly habit I have will remain with me. Yet, I can set an intention to embody the liberative possibility of choosing to live or act or show up in a unique way.

I can spiritually imagine and embody a future rich with the possibility of reemergence and rebirth by recalling that I, too, left Egypt, and so did we all. Our *sederim* are not meant to be rote, tired exercises in reciting lines that may not have meaning for us. They are, instead, about embodying the theological radicalism of our tradition. We move from degradation to praise, from narrowness to expanse in every generation, in large ways and in small ways. May it be so.

Rabbi Lauren Tuchman is a spiritual educator based in the Washington, DC area.

She is honored to call Rabbi Jonathan Slater a dear teacher for a number of years. His Torah studies to sustain the soul introduced and opened up for her the beauty of Hasidut.

Counting the Omer
From Diminishment to Expansiveness

Marcia Plumb

Counting the *Omer* is one of the most powerful rituals of transformation in my year. I love, and need, the seven week spiritual process of counting the days between *Pesach* and *Shavuot*. Each week focuses on a different *middah* (trait) as I practice it to hone and expand my soul. Rabbi Isaac Luria helped me understand why I feel more expansive after this spiritual 'retreat'. He taught that the word Pesach means skipping. "At the Exodus, Israel reached the highest state of mind (*gadlut*) before going through (hence skipping over) the lesser stages (*katnut*)."

The Children of Israel left Egypt on a spiritual high, in a state of fullness, wholeheartedness and openness. They needed the *gadlut* to lift them across the Reed Sea, and to overcome their spiritual weakness and lack of faith after 400 years of slavery. During their slavery, their spirits had shrunk into a state of *katnut* (diminishment). *Gadlut*, expansiveness, brings confidence. *Katnut* can be a result of fear. We shrink when we are afraid or uncertain. Journeying into the unknown, the Israelites needed confidence and hope to skip over the challenges of slavery and katnut, into freedom and gadlut.

Every year, at Pesach, we begin our journey from the tight narrow constricted place of *katnut–mitzrayim*. We unfold our *neshamot*, and expand them, day by day through the counting of the *omer*.

How do we do this? The Rebbe of Slonim, in *Netivot Shalom*, shows us that counting ("*sefartem*" ספרתם) refers to the word *sapir*, meaning light, illumination. Thus "u'*sefartem lachem*" – וספרתם לכם – comes to mean "create for yourselves illuminations") Every day that we count and practice the *middot*, we gain enlightenment. Each *sapir* opens our souls, bit by bit, day by day until we reach the Sinai of *gadlut*.

If we gain such a height of *gadlut*, why do we need to count the *Omer* every year? Why do we need to find that light every year? Because we have lived a whole year in between, in this crazy world. We have been beaten down by war, diminished by hatred and sin, and enslaved by feelings of powerlessness. *Pesach* releases and renews us back to hope and resiliency.

Every year, at *Pesach*, we go through the birth process. We relive our enslavement and time of constriction, followed by our release and freedom. Every year, when we come out of the birth waters, we have to expand from *katnut* to *gadlut*. Unlike the first Israelites however, we can't skip over any steps. We have to stretch our souls with painstaking care, day by day, *middah* by *middah*.

In order to embody our enlightenment and *gadlut*, I offer you this movement to do every day of the Omer. Bend forward from your waist with your head and arms dipping to the floor. Feel your body collapse inward into smallness. Then, slowly, vertebrae by vertebrae, lift your body up, bring your arms above your head, then open your arms out like wings, and widen your chest. Feel the new expansiveness.

May *Gadlut* be yours. Then expansiveness and "oneness will prevail above and below", and we will all sing a new song.

Rabbi Marcia Plumb is the senior rabbi of Congregation Mishkan Tefila, Brookline, MA. She is an experienced Mussar teacher and spiritual director.

Jonathan has been a gentle, loving and wise companion along her spiritual journey, as he has been to so many. His binah and hochmah (understanding and wisdom) has helped her grow from katnut to gadlut.

Lag B'Omer
The Point of Transition

Igal Harmelin

What is the origin of Lag B'Omer? Nobody really knows. The Talmud tells us that thousands of Rabbi Akiva's students died in a plague between Passover and Shavuot during the 49 days of *Sefirat Ha'omer*, the counting of the Omer. (Yevamot 62b) Later traditions held that the plague stopped on the 33rd day of the Omer (*Shulchan Arukh, Orakh Chayim, 491*). The number 33 in Hebrew numerology is "Lag" (ל"ג), so the name of the holiday literally means "the 33*rd* day of the Omer."

Days 1 through 32 of the Omer are characterized by sadness and mourning: no celebrations are allowed, neither trimming or cutting of hair (ibid). On the 33rd day there's a big reversal—bonfires are lit with great joy. The next 16 days are days of relief and excitement, leading to Shavuot, the celebration of the giving of the Torah.

The counting of the Omer is like a pendulum movement. For 32 days it moves towards sadness and loss; the 33rd day is the point of reversal, where the momentum shifts; and for 16 days it moves back towards the ultimate joy. Whereas physical pendulums move with equal energy in both directions, the period signifying sadness is twice as long as the period signifying joy. 32:16; which is 2:1.

The movement from 2 to 1, from duality to unity, echoes the movement from *Mitzrayim* (Egypt)—which literally means "duality of boundaries" or "bondage in duality"—to Canaan, the promised land of liberation. In Hebrew numerology, the word *Mitzrayim* (מצרים) has the numerical value of 380; Canaan (כנען) has the value of 190, exactly half. Again, 2:1.

Lag B'Omer is the point where the pendulum reverses direction. It is an other-worldly point of pure potentiality, where the rush towards duality has dissolved and the reverse movement towards unity has not yet started. It resembles the moment of suspension between the incoming breath and the outgoing breath, a brief moment just before the direction is reversed. There's another such moment, when the outgoing breath reaches its end and the direction is about to be reversed. These are very potent moments. Try this: devote an entire meditation session to gently noticing those points of suspension of your breath, at the end of inhalation and the end of exhalation.

As I write this, the momentum in the world seems to be towards duality and separation. Senseless killing in Eastern Europe has jolted the world into fear and alarm. But Lag B' Omer holds a promise: the dark movement towards duality and separation reaches an end. Just as the bonfires end the period of mourning, light can appear when darkness has exhausted itself. May the world have its Lag B'Omer moment soon. Amen.

Igal Harmelin is a spiritual director, trauma healer and a rabbinical student at the Aleph Ordination Program. Jonathan is an admired mentor, a brilliant chavruta (study partner) and a wise colleague.

Shavuot
Receiving Inner Torah, Here and Now

Sam Feinsmith

Me'or Eynaim, R. Menahem Nahum of Chernobyl, (trans. Rabbi Jonathan Slater)

ספר מאור עינים - פרשת וירא

"קיים אברהם אבינו ע"ה את כל התורה עד שלא ניתנה" (בבלי
יומא כח:). כי אורייתא מחכמה נפקא. וחכמה נקרא נקודה, ושם
כל התורה מלובש ומעוטף בנקודה אחד. ולכן היא "נעלמה מעיני
כל חי ומעוף השמים נסתרה" (איוב כח:כא), מאחר שכל התורה
כלולה בנקודה אחד. ולכן נאמר "וידבר אלקים את כל הדברים
האלה" (שמות כ:א), ודרשו רז"ל שאמר כל התורה כולה בדבור
אחד; שאמר כל התורה כמו שהיא בנקודה עליונה, שנקרא חכמה.
שהוא הי' של שם הוי"ה ב"ה.
אך מי יוכל להשיג כל התורה בנקודה אחד? לכן אמרו ישראל
"דבר אתה עמנו ונשמעה" (שמות כ:טז), שישתלשל ויבוא אל
הדעת, שהוא בחינת משה...

Abraham upheld the whole of the Torah even before
it was given" (B. Yoma 28b). Torah emerged from
Chokhmah (Wisdom), and that *sephirah* is depicted as
a point. There the whole of the Torah is garbed and
wrapped up in one point, and that is why "**it is hidden
from the eyes of all living, concealed from the fowl of
heaven**" (Job 28:21): it is contained totally within that
single point. So, when Scripture says "**God spoke** all
these words (*d'varim*)" (Ex. 20:1) the Sages interpret
saying that God expressed the whole of the Torah in
one speech-act (cf. *Mekhilta, Bachodesh* 4); God spoke
the whole of the Torah as It was in that supernal point,
called Wisdom. This is represented by the letter *yod* of
the Divine Name *HVY"H*.
But who can understand such a Torah, all in one point?

That is why the Israelites said to Moses, **"You speak to us and we will listen"** (Ex. 20:16): let it [this Torah] unfold and chain-down to *Da'at* (Awareness), which is embodied by Moses.

Rabbi Nahman of Bratzlav, *Likutei Moharan* 1:2 (trans. Rabbi Sam Feinsmith)

ליקוטי מוהר"ן א:ב

כִּי אִישׁ הַיִּשְׂרְאֵלִי צָרִיךְ תָּמִיד לְהִסְתַּכֵּל בְּהַשֵּׂכֶל שֶׁל כָּל דָּבָר, וּלְקַשֵּׁר עַצְמוֹ אֶל הַחָכְמָה וְהַשֵּׂכֶל שֶׁיֵּשׁ בְּכָל דָּבָר, כְּדֵי שֶׁיָּאִיר לוֹ הַשֵּׂכֶל שֶׁיֵּשׁ בְּכָל דָּבָר לְהִתְקָרֵב לְהַשֵּׁם יִתְבָּרַךְ עַל-יְדֵי אוֹתוֹ הַדָּבָר. כִּי הַשֵּׂכֶל הוּא אוֹר גָּדוֹל, וּמֵאִיר לוֹ בְּכָל דְּרָכָיו, כְּמוֹ שֶׁכָּתוּב, "חָכְמַת אָדָם תָּאִיר פָּנָיו" (קהלת ח:א).

For us Godwrestlers must always focus on the inner intelligence *(sekhel)* that lies within every object or event, and bind ourselves to the wisdom and inner intelligence that is to be found in each thing. This, so that the intelligence within each thing may illuminate for us how to draw closer to God through that object or event. For the inner intelligence is a great light that shines for us in all our ways, as is written, **"A person's wisdom causes her countenance to shine"** (Ecc. 8:1).

How might we receive Torah, here and now? If we understand and *experience* our own consciousness (*Da'at*) as a manifestation of the transcendent wisdom mind as the Rebbe from Chernobyl does, each moment of conscious living might transport us to the foot of Sinai anew. If we have trained our inner eye to look into the depth-dimension of reality as Rebbe Nahman instructs, we may come to discern in ourselves and all around us a kind of luminous "knowledge that frees [and coaxes] us to move…toward God" (Rose Mary Daugherty, *Discernment: A Path to Spiritual Awakening*).

Traditionally, Jews have related to the festival of Shavuot as a time for reenacting the giving of the Torah at Sinai and rededicating our-selves to the ongoing study of Scripture. The Hasidic teachings offer us a path to entering Shavuot as a moment for discovering an inner font of revelation, revitalizing our spiritual lives, and reigniting the flame of our desire for a living God. Even as we renew our motivation to engage in Torah study, we might also commit to returning daily to a practice of cultivating mindful awareness to deepen and expand our inner well of living Torah.

Practice:

Find a comfortable and supportive seat in a quiet place. Close your eyes or keep them open and downcast with a soft gaze. Adopt a relaxed, upright posture, allowing your body to be rooted and dignified like a mountain. Take a few deep, relaxing breaths and settle into stillness.

Next, spend some time cultivating awareness of the current of your breathing—where you feel it most prominently in your body. If the breath doesn't feel regulating, focus instead on sounds as they arise, change, and pass away. Even as you attend to these physical sensations, become aware of the innately spacious, inner space that knows your moment-to-moment experience. Notice how awareness keeps pouring into you. Feel its energy and pulse. Seek its source. Listen for its wisdom.

When you're ready, shift your attention to anything you'd like—the sight of the sky, the feeling of clothing on your body, or the scent of coffee coming from the kitchen. Shining your awareness and presence upon this phenomenon, invite the object to share its Torah with you. Notice what you notice. Feel what you feel.

Rabbi Sam Feinsmith is a Program Director and member of the core faculty at the Institute for Jewish Spirituality.

He loves and appreciates how Jonathan keeps his attention steadily trained on the work of drawing close to and being of service to the Divine in all things—and always with good humor.

Tisha be-Av
At the Crossroads
Mindfulness, Suffering, & Redemption

Barry Dolinger

How shall we confront the reality of pain and suffering spiritually? Given the cataclysms of our world, where is there any space to allow for the real possibility of redemption? Repentance? In other words, where is there room for empathic, mindful practice in a harsh world that seems so utterly distant from it all. Commenting on the conclusion of the Book of Lamentations, Levi Yitzhak of Berdichev offers a mesmerizing take:

> Another explanation for "take us back, YHVH, to You, and we will return; renew our days as of old."* What is the explanation of the words, "of old," in the context of this verse? . . . The explanation is thus. Every person in Israel is required to believe with full faith that in each and every moment, they receive vitality from the Blessed Creator, as the Rabbis expound: "Each soul (*neshama*) will praise Yah - each and every breath (*neshima*) will praise Yah."** For each moment, the vitality desires to leave a person, and the Blessed Holy One sends back new vitality. We find that it is according to this principle that repentance (*teshuvah*) works for every single human being. When a human being engages in repentance, they demonstrate belief that they are, at that moment, an entirely new creation, and Hashem, may God be Blessed, in God's abundant mercy, doesn't recall the prior sins. But if, God forbid, a person does not believe in this, then repentance won't work, God forbid.

---

* Lamentations 5:21

** Bereishit Rabbah 11

This is the explanation of the *midrash*, "every mention of the word, 'now' [in the Torah] denotes repentance." Since a person believes that they are *now* a new person, repentance operates successfully. This is the explanation of the verse, "take us back, YHVH, to You, and we will return"... How will a person return? By having their days renewed like old. This explains the [cryptic] passage of Talmud, "when are you [the messiah] coming? He replied, today. 'Today, if you heed His voice.'"* — when you live with this quality that each day you are an entirely new creation.**

There is a two-step move here. First, how can we repent or change individually? By renewing our days as of old. But wait! Are the days new, and we're meant to put the past behind us, or are we supposed to yearn for a supposedly more innocent past? In the past, says R' Levi Yitzhak, the spiritual masters practiced mindfulness, living in the present, and not the past. It's a paradox. Repentance is fundamentally rooted in a practice of *now/עתה*, of being mindfully attuned to the present situation and having enough awareness of this reality to escape the accumulated anxiety and trauma that inhibits real change.

Secondly, the ramifications are not localized, because all of a reality is an interconnected unity. In the Talmudic passage cited, the Messiah is distinguished for bandaging only one individual at a time; others treat many patients at once. The messiah is a healer fully engrossed in practicing local acts of empathy, wholly attuned to the pain of individuals. Our global problems are not served by quickly scaling up, but rather by harnessing empathic awareness and healing fully. This is what it means to "listen" to the voice of the Creator. By attuning ourselves to the newness of each present moment with connection and empathy for the suffering of others, we transcend *churban*/destruction together.

---

* Talmud *Sanhedrin* 58a

** *Kedushat Levi. Megillat Eicha* 16.a

Rabbi Barry Dolinger lives in Providence, Rhode Island, with his wife Naomi and two daughters, Netzach and Yahli.

One of the many things he most admires about Jonathan is his ability to listen and understand, and then support or challenge, occupying the twin roles of loving friend and honest mentor (or even a type of guru!) with grace and effect. There are few other people whose feedback is as valuable to me personally.

Tu be-Av
'Yearning to Breathe Free'

Laurie E. Green

From every human being there rises a light that reaches straight to heaven, and when two souls that are destined to be together find each other, the streams of light flow together and a single brighter light goes forth from that united being.
The Baal Shem Tov

In Hasidic tradition, romantic love is a manifestation of Divine love. A direct experience of God's love for us would be too overwhelming for us to experience, so God manifests Godself in a specific person or object of attraction. It is this pure love which entices us every day of the year, but especially on Tu be-Av.

Upon my couch at night
I sought the one I love –
I sought, but found him not...
– Song of Songs 3:4

I grieve for you,
My brother Jonathan,
You were most dear to me.
Your love was wonderful to me
More than the love of women.
– II Samuel 1:26

On Tu be-Av, this joyous day of romantic love and ecstatic dancing, let us celebrate the unsung loves of our people. I dedicate this teaching to all unknown queer lovers and their queer, Jewish love poetry. Thus, I share with you a section of the more recently discovered work of, perhaps, the most famous Jewish Lesbian poet – Emma Lazarus.

"Assurance," Emma Lazarus

Last night I slept, & when I woke her kiss
Still floated on my lips. For we had strayed
Together in my dream, through some dim glade,
Where the shy moonbeams scarce dared light our bliss,
The air was dank with dew, between the trees,
The hidden glow-worms kindled & were spent.
Cheek pressed to cheek, the cool, the hot night-breeze
Mingled our hair, our breath, & came & went,
As sporting with our passion. Low & deep...

Cultivating our ability to receive love, and to give love, is of great importance to my spiritual practice. You may wish to try this meditation. Slowly breathe in and out, at your own pace. All the lost loves, I take into my heart. All the broken hearts I release as I breathe out. All the unknown love poems, they fill my lungs. (Breathe out). All the secret lovers, they are with me. (Breathe out).

Rabbi Laurie E. Green is an educator, author, activist and yoga instructor.
Jonathan's love for Torah, and even more for his students, taught her much about love, as a parent, a student, a teacher, a partner, and in so many other ways.

Rosh Hashanah
Finding the Good Sparks

David Lerner

Each year is a struggle.

With the beginning of Elul, I find myself attempting to engage in *teshuvah* - in a serious process of repentance as we build toward Rosh Hashanah. While there are many names for the Jewish new year, *Yom Hadin* (the Day of Judgment) is the one that resonates with the High Holiday liturgy. While we may not fully believe that God is sitting inscribing people in the book of life, many of us feel that we are engaged in a holy process of self-evaluation and change.

At times, I find myself lost in this process.

Reciting Psalm 27 and hearing the shofar during the month before Rosh Hashanah awaken me and gird me for this work.

But how do I actually do it?

The Yiddish writer Y. L. Peretz in his amazing story "If Not Higher" describes a rabbi who secretly goes out during the *Aseret Yemei T'shuvah* (the Ten Days of Repentance) to take care of an elderly woman. The lesson is that helping others can be the key to transforming ourselves.

Rabbi Nahman of Bratzlav (*Likutei MoHaRan* 282) offers one of the most compelling and insightful teachings on this topic. He writes that we should start the process of *teshuvah* by remembering that we have to judge others *l'khaf zekhut* (giving them the benefit of the doubt) in the words of *Pirkei Avot*. Rebbe Nahman encourages us to try to find some goodness even within someone who is challenging or who we feel is not a good person.

Find even a small spark of goodness in them and help them see that. From that *"me'at tov* - little bit of good" (translation by Rabbi Art Green), we can start on a new transformational journey that can change our lives.

Rebbe Nahman does not end his teaching there, Instead, he encourages us to do the same for ourselves.

This may be even harder!

The process of *teshuvah* can be overwhelming. Sometimes, we cannot change since we are too hard on ourselves. However, if we try the practice of searching for the little spark of goodness within ourselves, we "can change our whole life, [bringing] ourselves to *teshuvah.*"

As Rosh Hashanah approaches, I try to use this technique of focusing on the good in others each day, even toward people who may be challenging for me. After I find their spark of goodness, I spend some time thinking of a good aspect of myself.

While this process remains demanding, it holds the promise that we can change our relationships with others and, most especially, with ourselves.

Rabbi David Lerner is the senior rabbi of Temple Emunah in Lexington, MA and one of the founders of the Community Hevra Kadisha of Greater Boston and Emunat HaLev – the Meditation Institute of Temple Emunah.

Jonathan has been a thoughtful, caring, generous and kind presence on his spiritual journey over two decades. Jonathan's ability to listen and gently guide him through mindfulness practice, halakhah, and Hasidic texts has been a boon to him and his community. He is grateful to call Jonathan "Mori V'Rabi – my rabbi and teacher."

Yom Kippur
Blessing the Sacred Adversary

Rabba Kaya Stern-Kaufman

On Yom Kippur we enter deeply into the crucible of our own souls. There is no more hiding. Our traditional prayers and practices encourage an encounter with the truth about ourselves so as to begin a process of repair. Our *viddui* (confession) practice of reciting all the ways we have erred lays out a path for growing self-awareness and ultimately for forgiveness of oneself and of others. Yom Kippur provides an opportunity to cleanse the mind and heart from the dross of anger, resentment, and judgement. A new beginning.

As lovely as this sounds, we all encounter some people that are difficult to forgive or difficult to love; people that get under our skin, try our patience and aggravate us to no end.

Regarding this, Rabbi Yaakov Yoseph of Polnoye, a direct disciple of the Baal Shem Tov, taught that when we encounter some aspect in another person that appears ugly or unappealing, we must recognize that these qualities are only recognizable to us because they reside within us. *

Pre-dating Sigmund Freud by 200 years, he deftly describes the phenomenon of projection, but adds a spiritual insight. That person who calls to mind such unappealing qualities within ourselves, is presenting us with a gift. For here is a great opportunity for *teshuvah*, to transform these qualities within ourselves.

The first challenge is to recognize that we share qualities with the ones who aggravate us the most. This is likely why they aggravate us so intensely. With this awareness, it is possible to move from an attitude of judgment to a recognition of our shared humanity. From this place, compassion becomes possible, both for oneself and for the person who has brought us this gift.

R. Yaakov Yosef goes on to say that this is the deeper meaning of

---

*   *Toldot Yaakov Yosef, Vayetze #5* and *Chayye Sarah #2* the phrase: *Shiviti Adonai l'negdi tamid* - I place (the recognition of) God before me always (Ps. 16:8). He reads:

Shiviti Adonai — **I place** (the recognition of) **God,** *b'negdut,* in the situations and people that appear in opposition to me. We might also rename that challenging person as the sacred adversary. In recognizing the gift of greater self-awareness, brought by the sacred adversary, we can even develop compassion and thereby, change our responses to others.

This is true *teshuvah*. In this way we return to ourselves as the source of the reality in which we live. We open a compassionate heart, bringing more peace to our relationships and to the world we create.

Practice, based on the Ho'oponopono Forgiveness Practice:

Find a comfortable seat. Pay attention to your in-breath and your out-breath.

Place your hands on your heart, directing your attention to yourself and recite the following slowly 3 times:

> I am sorry
> I forgive you
> I love you
> I thank you

Call to mind someone you wish to forgive. Hold their image in your mind's eye and imagine that person stands before you.

Recite and seek out the following:

> Source of Creation, help me see the qualities I share with this person.

Continue to see this person standing before you and recite the following slowly three times:

> I am sorry
> I forgive you
> I see your pure soul

I thank you

Release the person.
Release yourself.

Rabba Kaya Stern-Kaufman is Rabbi of Temple Israel in Portsmouth NH.

She has been deeply inspired by Jonathan's clarity of presence, his compassion and generosity of heart.

Sukkot
Dwelling in Life's Transient Beauty

Tracy Nathan

One autumn day, my junior high math teacher wrote on the board with each word in a different shade of colored chalk: "This is the first day of the most beautiful week of the year."

He wanted us to notice and appreciate the spectacular beauty that in a few days would be gone. In the northern hemisphere, we celebrate Sukkot during this time of fleeting beauty, and we read the book of Kohelet with the well-known refrain: הֲבֵל הֲבָלִים הַכֹּל הָבֶל.

The word הֶבֶל is Kohelet's central motif, and it expresses something that we poignantly sense during this time of year: the fleeting nature of life and all its beauty. הֶבֶל comes from the word for vapor or breath. The many translations of this word betray the fears that the author and readers struggle with: "Vanity," "Futility," "Meaningless," "Senseless." And yet, how can a Jewish book call life senseless and meaningless?

As the author of Kohelet contemplates his mortality, what he understands is that life is transient. We may believe we will gain immortality through the acquisition of things and the building of monuments but in fact, it is all transient. He realizes that the key to dealing with this is not to deny this transience but rather to embrace it and understand that within it lies the meaningfulness of life.

This is how Rabbi Mordechai Joseph Leiner, the Ishbitzer Rebbe, understands why we read Kohelet on Sukkot:

ושמעתי דלכן קורין אותו בסוכות, לא מפני שמהביל שמחת עולם הזה, רק שממנו נקח תוקף ועיקר השמחה האמיתית ע"י ההבלת כל עניני עולם הזה

And I heard that this is why we read it on Sukkot: not in order to make insubstantial the joys of this world, but rather, we take from it the power and essence of true joy, by means of the transitory nature of everything in this world.

The world is not meaningless but it is fleeting. If we all went on forever, one might not live in *this* precious moment.

Sukkot, too, is about recognizing what is both precious and perishable. The experience of moving out of our permanent dwellings and moving into the Sukkah - an impermanent shelter - guides us in our practice of embracing the meaning and even the joy to be found within the transience. We are commanded לֵישֵׁב בְּסוּכָּה, to dwell in the Sukkah, to sit with the impermanence and to focus our attention on the joy and blessing to be found right now, in this very moment. As you recite the blessing of dwelling in the Sukkah, I invite you to fully and truly dwell in this very moment, brimming with life and joy.

Rabbi Tracy Nathan teaches at Saul Mirowitz Jewish Community Day School in St. Louis, MO and is in the fourth cohort of the IJS Clergy Leadership Program.

Jonathan is a model teacher for her of authenticity, humility, and openheartedness.

Hanukkah
Wholeness
Resting in 'Thus'

Margie Jacobs

"We are taught that although there was sufficient oil to burn for only one day, it lasted eight days... This does not have to be seen only in temporal terms. "Eight" represents wholeness..."
—Rabbi Yehuda Aryeh Lieb of Ger, *Sefat Emet**

In Jewish numerology, six is associated with creativity and creation. The world was created in six days, and on the seventh day, God rested. Similarly, we work to bring tikkun to our incomplete and imperfect world during the week. On Shabbat, the seventh day, we pause to rest and be restored. While seven is a number of completion—a pause *within* the cycle of time— the number eight is beyond or outside of time. With its infinite loop, the number 8 is, as the *Sefat Emet* says, a symbol of wholeness. The number eight invites us to enter a realm in which everything is exactly as it should be – limitless, unchanging, a wholeness (*shleimut*) that reflects and generates a deep peace (*shalom*). This is the realm that we enter during the eight days of Hanukkah.

The *Sefat Emet* also teaches that the word "Hanukkah" can be divided into two separate words, *"hanu"* – they camped (or rested) – and *"kah"* or *"koh"* – thus. From a mindfulness perspective, we might understand this as an invitation to "rest in thus" – to let go of the struggle to change what is true in this moment.

The *Sefat Emet* writes: "After the terrible struggles and battles against the Greek kingdom, they had no strength left to attain wholeness. God helped them, and the tiny point of holiness within them miraculously led them in an instant back to wholeness. Wholeness is the peace and rest of coming back to one's root."

Like our ancestors in the Hanukkah story, we may feel exhausted,

---

* Primary source translations by Dr. Arthur Green

broken, or "not enough." In lighting the Hanukkah candles, we too may illuminate a "tiny point of holiness," a part of ourselves that is eternal, unchanging, sacred, and whole.

Practice:

With lights dimmed, sit facing the lit Hanukkah candles. Notice the movement of the bright flames, dancing and changing in each moment. As you settle, rest your attention on the steady blue flame that fuels the brighter flame. Now turn your attention inward (with eyes open or closed), resting deeply as you receive each breath. As you settle even more, invite into your awareness a tiny point of holiness within, your own root or source. This place may feel quiet, calm, eternal, bright, or whole.

In whichever way you experience this point within, let your attention rest there. If you experience difficult emotions or bodily aches, gently and with compassion acknowledge them and return to this innermost point (*nekudah penimit*). Invite your body and your breath to soften, allowing this point to expand so that it illuminates and fills your entire body. Rest in the wholeness of coming back to your source.

Rabbi Margie Jacobs participated in the second cohort of the IJS Rabbinic Leadership Program and is a facilitator of the Jewish Studio Process. She has served as a congregational rabbi and as a regional director for IJS.

Jonathan holds the world of Hasidic text in his mind and memory like no one she has encountered. At a moment's notice, he offers himself with joy and generosity as a key to this world for all of us who call on him.

Shemitah
I - Thou, I – It

Hasha Musha Perman

Shemitah means release. It is a mitzvah and a spiritual practice.

Exodus 15:10-11:

וְשֵׁשׁ שָׁנִים תִּזְרַע אֶת־אַרְצֶךָ וְאָסַפְתָּ אֶת־תְּבוּאָתָהּ:

Six years you shall sow your land and gather in its yield;

וְהַשְּׁבִיעִ֞ת תִּשְׁמְטֶ֣נָּה וּנְטַשְׁתָּ֗הּ וְאָֽכְלוּ֙ אֶבְיֹנֵ֣י עַמֶּ֔ךָ וְיִתְרָ֕ם תֹּאכַ֖ל חַיַּ֣ת
הַשָּׂדֶ֑ה כֵּן־תַּעֲשֶׂ֥ה לְכַרְמְךָ֖ לְזֵיתֶֽךָ:

but in the seventh you shall let it rest and lie fallow. Let the needy among your people eat of it, and what they leave let the wild beasts eat. You shall do the same with your vineyards and your olive groves.

Cultivate awe instead of planting. Let go of control. Love the unknown. Cherish the earth and each other. A saying in Alcoholic Anonymous is *"Let go and let God"*.

Shemitah commands that we open our hearts, hands, and minds to "let the needy…and… the wild beasts eat," the time aware of our impulse to control and manipulate people, places, and things, for power and greed.

At the turn of the 20*th* century, Martin Buber led the Jewish renaissance as the "re-spiritualization of Judaism in diaspora," an effort that has been revived by the work of the IJS.

Shemitah is release from the objectification of life. *Shemitah* is a practice of opening to everything. Martin Buber describes I- THOU: "When we encounter another individual truly as a person, not as an object for use, we become fully human."

Shemitah frames the It of I-IT, defined by Buber: "The I-IT encounter relates to another as object, completely outside of ourselves."

The It is a product of alienation, in contrast to the loving potential and rejuvenating energy that *Shemitah* offers. "Who only lives with that (IT) is not human."

Shemitah invites us to release manipulation and control, and ultimately, practice new behaviors that enhance loving relationships. Buber: "Love is responsibility of an I for a THOU – the equality of lovers."

Questions for further thought:

1. When do you experience power struggles? How can you release control and increase love?
2. What habit(s) are you willing to release from your life?
3. What mitzvah can you add to your life?

Cantor Hasha Musha Perman, Congregation Beth Shalom, is a graduate of the first IJS Cantorial Leadership Cohort, who meandered from theatre, art, and music to a spiritual practice grounded in awareness, compassion, and love.

Her dear friend Jonathan is the gentle voice of wisdom accompanied by the light laughter of mutual understanding. He willingly shares his personal experience to deepen and open the heart. He practices what he preaches, but he is no preacher.

Always Walking in God

Sylvia Boorstein

> Always consider in your heart that you are close to the blessed Creator, that God surrounds you from every side. Be so attached that you no longer have to keep settling with yourself that you are close to God. See the blessed Creator with your mind's eye; [see] that God is "the place of the world." This means that God was there before creation and that the world stands within the Creator.
>
> Be so attached that the main thing you see is the blessed Creator, rather than looking first at the world and only secondarily at God. God should be the main thing you see.
>
> Consider that the Creator is endless, surrounding all the worlds. But God's blessed influx reaches down through the channels and flows into all worlds. We are always walking in God; we could not make a single movement without the divine flow and life-force.
>
> —**R. Levi Yitzhak of Berdichev's** *Kedushat Levi*

In the 1970s, when contemplative practices were newly in vogue in the United States, the practice that is now called Mindfulness was called Vipassana, literally a "special, super, seeing", a Buddhist term that is often translated as "insight". The three insights that one hopes to experience, viscerally and transformatively, are temporality, the ubiquitous nature of suffering in life and interconnectedness. The promised result of this "clear seeing" is the habituation of the mind, through wisdom, to equanimity and compassion for all beings.

Impermanence rang true for me when I first heard it as an "Insight." Even forty-three years ago, when I first heard it, my baseline melancholia—how fast life whizzes by—felt true. Suffering that comes with any loss of what is dear—deaths of kin, failed hopes and dreams, waning vitality—build exponentially as attachments expand

and years pass. I always knew that, I suppose, but it never seemed truer than now. The third insight, the insight of interconnectedness, I *sort* of knew. I could talk about the Thich Nhat Hahn poem about being both the boat captain and the child whose death he caused, or people who pray for the souls of people who harmed them, and, I momentary "get" that. I could say, "Because of that, this," (things have causes), but the further step, "Everything causes everything," should, if I really, *really* could hold it in my mind, arouse equanimity in my mind, and compassion. Everything causes everything and is part of ongoing, ever-changing Creation. Everything that I do, everything that anyone does, is part of the endless unfolding. What I do matters. What everyone does matters, and no one is in charge.

I heard the R. Levi Yitzhak teaching from the rabbi at Congregation Beth Ami in Santa Rosa, California, twenty-five years ago. I remember thinking, and *feeling*, "If I speak, it is God speaking. If I lift my arm, it is God lifting." I have not forgotten that feeling. It is incremental in what I hope is the continuing consolidation of my understanding.

Sylvia Boorstein, is the co-founding teacher of Spirit Rock Meditation Center in Woodacre, CA, and part of the initial teaching faculty of the Institute for Jewish Spirituality. Jonathon Slater was the rabbi at Congregation Beth Ami who shared the R. Levi Yitzhak teaching with her. He continues to be one of her dearest friends.

The Order of Creation

Nancy Flam

Hasidism, as a popular movement of mystical revival, highlighted the inner life as a central locus of religious practice. We inheritors of that tradition work to internalize its language and teachings, and then transmit and transform them as we create and express what has come to be called Neo-Hasidism*. As post-moderns, we discern what to draw forward and what to leave behind from the men who articulated, lived and taught the original Hasidism in 18th, 19th and 20th century Europe. Surely, we aim to advance teachings that illuminate the inner life, as well as devotional and contemplative practices to cultivate the mind and heart to realize the oneness of Being. But leading Neo-Hasidic thinkers such as Rabbis Zalman Schachter-Shalomi and Arthur Green who paved the path for Neo-Hasidic expression in America have taught us to leave behind, for example, Hasidism's generally fearful and demeaning attitudes toward women and non-Jews.

We detect here a movement toward greater inclusivity and dignity for all people. In that spirit, I suggest that as Neo-Hasidic thinking and practice develops, we extend that inclusivity to all beings, and not just human beings.** Such a commitment would surely challenge

---

* A century ago, a number of modern European Jews sought to bring forth essential insights and teachings of Hasidism through their writing and teaching in order to share them with others outside of Hasidic communities. This effort, known as Neo-Hasidism, then extended to America and also to Israel where such work continues to this day. See *A New Hasidism: Roots* and *A New Hasidism: Branches*, edited by Arthur Green and Ariel Evan Mayse (Philadelphia: The Jewish Publication Society, 2019).

** There is a deeply universalizing strand within the tradition, but it is often not highlighted as central. Remember that Adam was created as a single, androgenous human being (Gen. 1:27) so that no one might say "my father is greater than yours" (Mishnah Sanhedrin 4:5, B. Sanhedrin 37a). Adam was made from dust gathered from the four corners of the earth so that no one might say "the dust of the body of Adam is mine [alone]" (Midrash Tanhuma, Pekudei 3). Even the mosquito was created before

familiar Jewish assumptions about the place of the human being, and the Jew in particular, within creation.

It seems to me that all subjects reflexively experience themselves as "the center of the world," and for humans, this pertains not only in infancy, childhood and adolescence. Throughout our lives, the world impinges on *these* ears, *these* eyes, *this* body, *this* heart, *this* mind. Navigating our lives through the senses, we actually *do* experience ourselves as the center of the world. It takes reflective thought, training and commitment to recognize and honor other beings as subjects, each the center of their own worlds. The mitzvah to "Love your neighbor as yourself" reminds us that the world is composed of manifold subjects, and so trains us to think and act in ways that mitigate the optical delusion of our own individual, existential centrality.

Peoples, not only people, think of themselves as the center of the world, too. Deeply inscribed within the Jewish psyche is the central role of the Jewish nation and its activity in the world. Within Jewish mystical life, in particular, the world and its renewal are understood to depend upon the devotional activity of Jews engaged in prayer and other mitzvot. Directed prayer and contemplation repair the cosmic breach, uniting heaven and earth, ensuring that the flow of vital energy continues to water the earth.

Moreover, the rabbis teach that it was for the sake of Israel that creation came into being.* While such a view might beneficially shore up a Jew's sense of agency, mission and value in the world and so inspire great works of thought, devotion and action, it might also quite insidiously give rise to a lesser estimation of other peoples and created beings.

Hasidism in Context

Hasidism was born at the same time as the dawn of the Industrial Revolution. Over the years, Hasidic leaders would respond to fundamental challenges of the enlightenment, secularism and nationalism, as well as some of the pressures the industrial revolution made on

---

humans, reminding humans not to be haughty (Sanhedrin 38a). For an exquisite paean to God about creation and its interconnectivity, see Psalm 104.

* ב–ראשית: For the sake of "reysheet", and Israel is known as "reysheet." See Rashi on Genesis 1:1.

the working person. However, they did not – could not - respond to the planetary threat only recently understood as the result of burning massive amounts of fossil fuels which drove, and drives still, industrial societies throughout the world. I believe that if Hasidism is to be relevant to life in the Anthropocene, its Neo proponents must dedicate significant thinking and action to this overwhelming planetary challenge.

A central tenet of Hasidism is that all of creation is holy: *Melo khol ha'aretz kevodo.* ("All the earth is filled with God's presence."**) There is no place that is devoid of God. This understanding derives from a mystical cosmogony that posits a process of emanation from God's boundless Nothingness (*Ein Sof, Ayin*) to a concatenation of "worlds," or dimensions of being, all the way down to the physical world which we know with our senses. In an emanationist view, one understands that the Creator is never separate from Its creation, in the same way that the sun is not separate from its rays. Godliness can be found everywhere, because God is the essence of all manifestation. Furthermore, within creation, it is claimed, there is no transformation of essence, only of form.*** Only the divine being is real. To recognize the non-

---

** Isaiah 6:3

*** "Concerning the essential theme of the unity of the Holy One: He is called One and Unique, and 'all believe that He is all alone,' exactly as He was before the world and was created when He was all alone, as it is written, 'Thou wast the same before the world was created; Thou hast been the same since the world was created.' This means exactly the same, without any change, as it is written, *For I the Lord have not changed* (Mal. 3:6).

"Neither this world nor the supernal worlds effect any change in God's unity by their having been created *ex nihilo.* Just as He was all alone, single and unique before they were created, so He is one and alone, single and unique now that they have been created, since beside Him everything is a nothing, absolutely null and void. For the coming into being of all the upper and lower worlds out of nonbeing, the vital power that sustains them [and prevents them] from reverting to their previous states of nonexistence and nothingness is but the word of God and the breath of His mouth that is clothed in them. The nature of the divine order is not like that of a creature of flesh and blood. When man utters a word, the breath emitted in speaking is something that can be sensed and perceived as a thing apart from him, separate from its source, i.e., the ten faculties of soul.

"However, the speech of the Holy One is not, heaven forbid, separated from Him, for there is nothing outside of Him and there is no place devoid of Him... God's speech and thoughts are absolutely at one with his essence and being, even after His speech has been actualized in the creation of the worlds, just as it was united with Him

substantiality of the material world in the light of the divine reality is a matter of training one's perception through study, contemplation and prayer.*

If such a practice, known as apprehending the "upper unity," requires seclusion of the senses into an absorptive state of singular focus on the unmanifest reality of God, then the parallel work of the "lower unity" is to contemplate each and every particular of creation as a unique expression of the holy life-force (*chayyut*).** The granite, the limestone, the fungus, the tree, the amoeba, the ant, the caterpillar, the fish, the frog, the antelope, as well as the human are all equally unique expressions of the one life-force, the Holy One of Being. To contemplate them is to know God as God manifests in riotous variety; it is to receive God's expression (ex-pression, that is, what is pressed out from God's essence),

---

before the worlds were created. Thus, there is no change at all in His self, but only for the created beings which receive their life-force from His word." R Shneur Zalman of Liadi, *Tanya*, *Likutei Amarim*, chapters 20 – 21.

* As Rabbi Shneur Zalman of Liadi, explains: "The worlds are annihilated in utter annihilation to Him, may He be praised… and this is the upper unity where the absolute *Ayin* resides… and all of it is esteemed as naught before Him, and everything is like the forgoing… for the whole corporeal world and all the corporeal things in it are complete nullity and nothing at all… Therefore, this is the true worship, to divest one's mind, one's heart from all corporeality." Rabbi Shneur Zalman of Liadi, *Boneh Yerushalayim*, p. 15. Quoted from Rachel Elior, *The Paradoxical Ascent to God: The Kabbalistic Theosophy of Habad Hasidism*. (Albany, NY: State University of New York Press, 1993), 28 – 29.

** "Here we encounter God's oneness *in* and *through* the world, not despite it. Each flower, each blade of grass, each human soul, is a new manifestation of divinity, a new unfolding of the cosmic One that ever reveals itself through its multicolored garments, in each moment taking on new and ever-changing forms of life. In the variety of life's riches, we discover the unity that flows through them all, the divine life that animates all of being. Here the power and oneness of God are manifest in each of the lowliest and simplest forms of being, including the inanimate, as well as they are in the most magnificent and complex creations of the human mind. Each of them, real and distinctive in itself, bears witness to the single force of being that animates and unites them all. Existence here is celebrated in variety, in specificity, rather than in vast sameness. This God too represents infinity, but the infinity of One-in-many. 'The whole *earth* is filled with God's glory'" Arthur Green, *Seek My Face: A Jewish Mystical Theology*. (Woodstock, VT: Jewish Lights Publishing), 5

or, as the tradition might say, to hear God's speech.

I believe that this moment in history calls us Jews to the deep, devotional work of the lower unity. While Nothingness may be the ultimate reality that gives birth to all form, recognizing the Godliness that *is* creation might inspire the reverence and love that is needed to reconfigure our understanding of our location on the planet and our responsibility for its welfare.

Love and Awe

To contemplate deeply the particulars of creation has the potential to give rise to the two root spiritual sensibilities articulated in Torah, the Siddur and other Jewish literature: love and awe.*** These are the central devotional qualities we desperately need today to cultivate not only in relation to God, but also in relation to God's created world. Regarding love, we would say that such love expresses a sense of connection, a feeling of attraction to all that is, a kind of kinship, knowing ourselves to be part of and to belong to all of being. The plants are, in point of fact, our ancient relatives. "All green plants are our ancestors and our makers. If you love your maker, you love plants (and hydrogen, and electromagnetism). The energy that enters into chemical bonds during photosynthesis in green cells eventually becomes us."**** We humans are not separate from the more-than-human world; rather, we are all, quite literally, related.

"Contemplate the wonders of creation," Rav Kook exhorted, "the divine dimension of their being, **not as a dim configuration that is presented to you from the distance but as the reality in which you live.** Know yourself and your world . . . find the source of your own life, and of the life beyond you, around you, the glorious splendor of the life in which you have your being. The love that is astir in you – raise it to its basic potency and its noblest beauty, extend it to all its dimensions, toward every manifestation of the soul that sustains the universe . . ."*****

*** See, for example, Deut.10:12, the *Ahavah Rabbah* prayer, and Maimonides in *Yesodei HaTorah*, 1 -2.

**** Paul R. Fleischman, *Wonder: When and Why the World Appears Radiant.* (Amherst, MA: Small Batch Books, 2013), 202.

***** Kook, Abraham Isaac. *Abraham Isaac Kook.* Ben Zion Bokser, trans. (New York: Paulist Press, 1978), 207; emphasis added.

In addition to such love and kinship, contemplating creation might lead to a tremendous sense of awe in the face of its complexity, mystery and grandeur. Modern cosmologists and astronomers speak of time and space in terms of billions, something nearly impossible for us to imagine. The universe is over *thirteen billion* years old. Our galaxy is made of *100 billion* stars. And beyond the Milky Way, there are *billions of other galaxies*. (To consider: if we counted to just one billion, counting once per second, it would take us fifty years of continuous counting!) "God, what are we that you are mindful of us?"* We are so small, so transitory in the face of Heaven. And yet, the spiritual sense of awe we realize in any moment can connect us to the ultimate, to the ineffable, that is, to God, right here and right now.**

The secret of the "lower unity" is that it is not just the grand scale that might engender awe. Awe is generated through wonder at the way in which God creates and infuses each and every particular, as we perceive "a world in a grain of sand and Heaven in a wildflower."*** Each particular is testimony to the Source of all. As Abraham Joshua Heschel wrote: "Awe is more than an emotion; it is a way of understanding, insight into a meaning greater than ourselves. The beginning of awe is wonder, and the beginning of wisdom is awe. **Awe is an intuition for the dignity of all things, a realization that things not only are what they are but also stand, however remotely, for something supreme.**

---

* Psalm 8:5.

** Here is a delightful description of the experience of awe that includes contemplation of both what is beyond and what is within us as part of the same unfathomable reality:

"...[W]e stopped to look at the stars. And as usual, I felt in awe. And then I felt even deeper in awe at this capacity we have to be in awe about something.

"Then I became even more awestruck at the thought that I was, in some small way, a part of that which I was in awe about.

"And this feeling went on and on... 'awe infinitum.'

"And I felt so good inside and my heart felt so full, I decided I would set time aside each day to do awe-robics.

"Because at the moment you are most in awe of all there is about life that you don't understand, you are closer to understanding it all than at any other time." Jane Wagner, *The Search for Signs of Intelligent Life in the Universe*. (New York: Harper & Row, 1986).

*** William Blake, from "Auguries of Innocence." *Poets of the English Language* (Viking Press, 1950).

Awe is a sense for transcendence, for the reference everywhere to mystery beyond all things. It enables us to perceive in the world intimations of the divine, to sense in small things the beginning of infinite significance, to sense the ultimate in the common and the simple: to feel in the rush of the passing the stillness of the eternal. What we cannot comprehend by analysis, we become aware of in awe."****

Absolutely everything is an expression of the ultimate. We can know this through deep contemplation of particulars.

Seder HaHishtalshelut

Contemplation of "Seder *HaHishtalshelut*,"***** the order of the chain of emanation, has been a central practice within Chabad Hasidism for centuries. Contemplating the emanation of divinity from *Ein Sof*, to *Ohr Ein Sof*, to all the *sefirot* and worlds is meant to generate intimate knowing of the divine within and without, along with love and awe towards It. *Seder HaHishtalshelut* strikes moderns, however, as arcane, labyrinthine and convoluted. In our day, learning and contemplating evolutionary cosmology and biology *with devotional intent*, while complicated, might provide an alternative, or a companion means for cultivating love and awe towards creation and the ineffable Source that has brought it into being.

I am suggesting that evolutionary cosmology and biology can be understood as another, parallel language for divine emanation, for the great chain (*shalshelet*) of being: from the mystery of the moment before the Big Bang to the creation of all of material reality: an interconnected, divinely-infused kinship of forms.

Just as Jewish mystical thought, especially Chabad philosophy, tells us that the *Ayin* of *Ein Sof* and the *Yesh* of creation are not separate or different in essence, science tells us that "matter and energy appear to be very different, but they are twins from the same birthing event. At a deep level they are forms of each other." ******

**** Abraham Joshua Heschel, *Who Is Man?* (Stanford, CA: Stanford University Press, 1965), Ch. 5; emphasis **added.**

***** A full articulation of the *Seder HaHishtalshelut* can be found in *The Gate of Unity: Sha'ar HaYichud of the Mittler Rebbe*, translated and annotated by Rabbi Benjamin Walters (North Haven, CT: CreateSpace Independent Publishing Platform, 2004).

****** Fleischman, *op. cit.*, 159.

Furthermore, "We now have a reasonably good understanding, not only of how countless stars were born and have died to create the matter composing our world, but also how life has come to exist as a natural consequence of the evolution of matter. We can reliably trace a thread of knowledge linking the evolution of primal energy into elementary particles, the evolution of those particles into atoms, in turn of those atoms into stars and galaxies, the evolution of stars into heavy elements, and of those elements into the molecular building blocks of life, and furthermore the evolution of those molecules into life itself, of advanced life forms into intelligence, and of intelligent life into cultured and technological civilization."*

Here we have an alternative "*Seder HaHishtalshelut*" that proceeds in stages, just as the Lurianic cosmogony does. Except that from a contemporary scientific view, the stages proceed not from *Ein Sof* to *Ohr Ein Sof* and so on, but from "the particulate, to the galactic, to the stellar, to the planetary, to the chemical, to the biological, and then to the cultural."**

Might the devotional contemplation of such a process offer an alternative path for Neo-Hasidic practitioners to cultivate a deep and abiding love and awe of creation and Creator, one that speaks to modern sensibilities while still retaining the basic movement of traditional Hasidic understandings of divine emanation? Might it not lead us to a profound respect, awe and love for creation as inherently holy? And might not that lived sensibility affect not only our thoughts and emotions, but also, and critically, our actions?

The call of the Jewish mystic in all ages is to act for the sake of repair. "The kabbalist's goal is to become a living bridge, uniting heaven and earth, so that God may become equally manifest above and below, for the healing and redemption of all."***

So may it be for us.

---

* https://lweb.cfa.harvard.edu/~ejchaisson/cosmic_evolution/docs/fr_1/fr_1_site_summary.html

** Ibid.

*** Seth Brody, "Human Hands Dwell in Heavenly Heights: Contemplative Ascent and Theurgic Power in Thirteenth Century Kabbalah." In *Mystics of the Book: Themes Topics and Typologies*, edited by R. Herrera (New York: Peter Lang), 153.

Rabbi Nancy Flam is a pioneer in the fields of Jewish healing and spirituality. She co-founded the National Center for Jewish Healing, serving as its West Coast Director, and also the Institute for Jewish Spirituality, serving as its first Executive Director. She teaches and writes widely about Jewish spirituality and Neo-Hasidism, and maintains a robust spiritual direction practice for individuals.

Jonathan's Torah erudition is equaled by his devotion to service. It is well-known that he is always at the ready to reply to a vast number of students who reach out to him to identify sources, to explain difficult texts and ideas, and to help them make Jewish meaning. He is also devoted to easing suffering in whatever ways he can through heart-to-heart listening and pastoral presence, in addition to providing teachings to help people work with their embodied experience of constricted heart and mind. Throughout our decades of shared work together at the Institute, Jonathan was our rock: genuine, solid, constant, dependable, and embodying spiritual gravitas. We are forever grateful for all the gifts he shared for so many years with our community, and most fundamentally, for the gift of his loving being.

The Flag and the Trees
Degel Machaneh Ephraim on the Two Trees of Eden

Arthur Green

Franz Kafka, in one of the *Parables and Paradoxes* that my teacher Nahum N. Glatzer excerpted from his works, speaks of the universal human exile from Eden. Kafka says (I am paraphrasing) that the reason Adam and Eve were expelled from paradise is not because they ate of the Tree of Knowledge, but because they separated it from the Tree of Life.

Remarkably, virtually the same interpretation was offered by the Catalonian Kabbalist Rabbi Ezra of Gerona, some eight hundred year earlier. I wondered, when seeing the two, whether the Kabbalistic source could have influenced the twentieth century writer. I discovered that was impossible, as Gershom Scholem only published the German translation of that obscure manuscript well after Kafka's passing in 1924.

It turns out, however, that there is a brief reference to this notion in the Zohar as well, composed several decades after R. Ezra. "It is permitted to eat of them [the two trees] together. We have seen that Abraham, Isaac, Jacob, and all the prophets did so and lived. But this tree is the Tree of Death...Whoever takes of it alone will die. It is a deadly poison because it has been separated from life."

I have long used this metaphor of the two trees to describe the situation of the contemporary university, a place where knowledge is cut off from life. The university transmits knowledge and critical thinking, within limits, to advance our goals, to prepare us for professions, ultimately to earn a livelihood and achieve security. It does not do so "for life," to figure out what we are doing here on earth and how we might find meaning in our brief sojourns here. Rare are those who turn to universities in order to attain wisdom by which to live. Most likely they would be dismissed as fools. The separation between the two trees runs very deep in our world.

As far as I had known, this account of the sin of Eden was neglected in Jewish sources after the Zohar, largely in the face of much more drastic-sounding narratives. How happily surprised I was, therefore, to recently find a couple of references to this same idea in a well-known Hasidic work, *Degel Machaneh Ephraim*, by a grandson of the Ba'al Shem Tov, R. Moshe Hayyim Ephraim of Sudilkow (1748-1800). He discusses it in connection with a major theme throughout his work, that of the transformation of evil into good, which he sees as a key teaching of Hasidism and as central to his grandfather's legacy. In Ukrainian Hasidism it is reshaped into many teachings around the theme of ha'ala'at ha-middot, or what might be called the *mussar* element within Hasidism.

The major source is in *parashat Nitsavim*:

> "From the logger of your trees to your water-carrier (Deut. 29:10)." One might say that Moses is pointing out to all Israel how the repair for the first human's sin is carried forward. Abraham began this repair. Therefore, Scripture says of him: Y-H-W-H appeared to Abraham amid the terebinths of Mamre (Gen. 18:1)." This means that he restored the tree (*ilan/elon*) through which Adam sinned and rebelled (*mamreh/Mamre*) against Y-H-W-H. Adam sinned regarding the Tree of Knowledge, separating it from the Tree of Life. His [Abraham's] repair subsumed the Tree of Knowledge within the Tree of Life.
>
> This is similar to what I heard from my grandfather on the verse "Turn from evil and do good (Ps. 34:15)." Remove (*sur/haser*) the evil from evil and transform it into good...
>
> All of the patriarchs partook in this restoration until Moses came and completed it, and thus [it goes on] in every generation.
>
> This is the meaning of "From the logger of your trees"... Abraham our Father was the quality of compassion and love. In this way, he bound himself constantly [to those qualities], effecting repair and unity between the two trees, the Tree of Life and the Tree of Knowledge. "Your water-carrier' is Moses, who drew forth the waters of Torah and thus completed the repair.

This remarkable text may be taken as a comment on the role of religion in the history of human consciousness. Abraham, first among the faithful, and Moses, giver of the Teaching, heal the universal human wound of expulsion and alienation from the soul's Edenic home. The exile of Israel, so dominant in our people's narrative, is itself a historical re-creation of the universal human condition. Exile begins on the far side of the flaming sword that keeps us from that womb of existence where we felt so safe and nurtured by the unswerving presence of the God of Life. The restoration culminates in Moses, who brings forth a Teaching that recombines the act of intellectual pursuit (Tree of Knowledge) with an ultimate affirming of the value and love of life. Yet this re-linking of the two trees is never permanent or to be taken for granted. It must go on "in every generation." Indeed, here we are.

In this reading, the expulsion of humanity from paradise may not have been as much a divine punishment as it was the necessary result of separation between the trees, a curiosity to know that recognized no responsibility to sustain or nourish life. Eating of the Tree of Knowledge means wanting to know for its own sake, without asking the question of whether that knowledge will be sustaining or destructive of life. This freedom of intellectual curiosity undoubtedly has brought about much good in the history of human advancement. Indeed, one might say that both arts and sciences in the post-renaissance world needed to liberate themselves from the secondary role of affirming the truth of faith and scripture. But this advance of unbridled speculative inquiry has also brought us the microbiologist who works to create biological weapons, the chemist employed by the armaments industry, the philosopher or jurist who justifies racism and genocide, and the "neutral" university that supports (and indeed often gets rich on) all their work.

The *Degel* associates this insight, which he offers as his own, with the Ba'al Shem Tov's teaching on the redeeming and transformation of evil. "Turn from evil and do good" is quoted multiple times throughout this work and frequently in other works of the early Hasidic corpus. *Sur*, "turn" is understood as though it were in the *hif'il* construction, meaning "remove." It seems to refer to a two-stage process in confronting evil, whether in the outer world or in facing it as an inclination within one's own personality, the *yetser ha-ra'*. There is a hard core of evil that must first be separated out from the actual deed or temptation. This seems to be the malicious intent, whether toward a fellow-creature or toward God, in an act of rebellion. Once this element of true "evil" has been set aside, the rest may be uplifted or transformed to good.

This moral act of transforming evil into good is part of a broader complex of such transformations that indeed do play a very prominent role in the BeSHT's legacy. Intertwined with the moral, there are both magical and mystical aspects of this transformative activity. The setting for discussion of it is often that of contemplation of words and letters, so central to the BeSHT's intellectual worldview. He is frequently quoted on the power of the righteous to transpose the letters that underlie reality, such as transforming those of נגע, "affliction," into ענג, "joy," ריב, "conflict," into רבי, "master," שקר, "falsehood" into קשר, "connection." This is in part a contemplative undertaking, an aspect of "entering into the word." With these particular examples, it may reflect a change in attitude, the way one deals with certain situations. But this transformative process has magical implications as well, since the outer reality reflected by those designations is said to be transformed, not just the mind of the one who confronts them.

The possibility of uplifting or transforming evil in early Hasidism has to be seen in the broader context of the highly selective Hasidic appropriation of ideas, terms, and motifs from the vast body of Kabbalistic literature, much of which was well known by the creators of the new popular movement. A major part of the Kabbalistic legacy had to do with the vast realm of evil and demonic forces, their origin within the Godhead (since all must ultimately derive from the One), and their great array of powers in contravening the divine will and in leading humans to do the same. This is the area in which Kabbalah's mythical imagination is most fully developed. The demonic universe, arrayed against the forces of goodness and divinity, controls much of what takes place in the world in which we live. Despite the origin of all from within God, there is a strongly dualistic or gnostic element within Kabbalah, one that in later generations also penetrated the Jewish folk-imagination and gave birth to a much believed-in demonology.

Protection from evil spirits and defense against whispered curses were part of the regular stock-in-trade of *ba'aley shem*. Recent studies have shown the BeSHT was an active participant in this sort of ritual activity for protection against *dinim*, rather undefined but broadly feared forces of evil. These could be the result of one's own sins, but might also have been bought upon one (or upon a whole community) by wicked actors intentionally invoking the forces of evil. It is not clear how this inherited role as a *ba'al shem* lived side by side with his broader message, one that sought to minimize the dualistic aspect of Kabbalah. It seems that evil is something that needs to be "cleaned up" or "straightened out," possibly with the help of a *ba'al shem* or a *rebbe*, so that one can then go on to the task of living the life of appreciating divine goodness. His teaching at its root was an essentially optimistic and affirmative one. The transformative process described above involves a certain "signing on" to that optimistic vision. God is to be found everywhere; all that hides Him from us is our inability or unwillingness to open our eyes to see. Hasidic teaching is aimed at curing us of that failure, leading us to constant awareness of God's presence and arousing in us a desire to serve in multiple ways. Proverbs 3:6 "Know Him in all your ways" becomes a great watchword of Hasidism.

Hasidism replaces the Kabbalist's great concern over the origin of evil with a much more practical and personal focus on what can be done to uplift or transform it. Quoting such older sayings as "Nothing evil descends from heaven" or "All the Compassionate One does, He does for good," the Hasidic preachers took great pains to say that the original intent of all God has created must be good. The reason there is evil in the world is that humans (not independent demonic forces) have distorted elements of that creation, including a twisting or reordering of the letters of divine speech. This distortion began with the sin of Adam and is repeated and amplified by the wicked of each generation. But the holy letters themselves long to be redeemed from this "bewitched" state, and in doing so one is participating in a great act of *tikkun*, affecting the cosmic order as well as one's own situation.

God has sent *tsaddikim* into the world in order to help rectify that situation. "The blessed Holy One saw that the righteous were few, so He rose up and planted them throughout the generations." Their task is to edify those around them, both by teaching and by personal example, about how to subjugate evil to good, ultimately leading to the reunion of the two trees of Eden.

Because Hasidism is an inward-focused devotional mysticism (its interest is much more in psychology than cosmology), much of the discussion of good and evil is centered around the two *yetsarim* or inclinations that are said to be present and struggling within the human heart. While some other Hasidic masters make use of the tradition that the good inclination enters humans only at the age of puberty, while the "evil" (perhaps "selfish" or "needy" is really a better term) is there from birth, our *Degel* here depicts them as both innate. Not surprisingly, he discusses the need to distinguish between them and then ultimately to combine them, evil subsumed within good, just like the two trees, in his homily on the classic good and evil twin story of the Torah, the birth of Jacob and Esau:

"The children struggled within her and she said 'In that case, why am I?...(Gen. 25:22)." We may say that the Torah is hinting at a moral lesson. It is known that the human has two inclinations, one good and one evil. Humans were created for the purpose of attempting to make the evil urge over into good. This means serving blessed Y-H-W-H in all matters deriving from the evil inclination.

Thus our sages taught (*Avot* 4:1) " Who is wise? One who learns from the entire person." In the books of the holy rabbi of Polonnoye it says "even from the evil urge." It is known that "God made one thing opposite the other (Eccles. 7:14). This means that there are people who transform their good urge into evil, God forbid. But when God graciously makes them aware of their useless deeds, they become astonished at themselves. How might they have been able to serve Y-H-W-H when the good urge was strong, but now even it has turned to evil! If so, **why have I even come into this world**, if I have accomplished nothing of value and even wrought evil by my deeds?

Once coming to this awareness, you begin to investigate and seek out [the nature of] true divine service. Then Y-H-W-H responds by means of a messenger, a good and trusted friend. The messenger informs you that there is no surprise here, because you have not ever truly worshipped the Creator. What you sometimes thought was worship with awe and love was in fact a lie, the result of pride. Your efforts to serve had wrought no results, for you had not yet made a distinction or separation of evil from good.

That is the main goal: to be separated from evil and turn it into good, as in "Turn from evil and do [or "make] good (Ps. 34:15)." That means to try **to remove the evil from within evil and make it all into good**. Then the evil urge will be subjugated to the holy and it will be possible to serve blessed Y-H-W-H [even] in matters that derive from the side of the evil urge.

This removal of the evil kernel, here perhaps as much lust as it is malice, is the essential prerequisite for *'avodah be-gashmiyyut*, worship by means of corporeal things, a value taken more easily for granted by some other voices within early Hasidism. The *Degel* repeats in multiple sermons, and sometimes in very demanding terms, that this separation from the core of evil must take place before one dares to transform evil into good.

In another place he offers a concrete example of how this might be transformed into practice: "For example, if a thought of lust falls into your mind, know this is because its root is in *hesed*, [the cosmic source of all love], but there is no one [i.e. no means] to uplift it. Therefore, be strong as a lion to do *hesed* with the *shekhinah* by means of charity, acts of lovingkindness, and other matters. This is the meaning of חסיד המתחסד עם קונו איזהו "Who is a *hasid*? One who acts with *hesed* toward his Master." It is not God who needs our *hesed*, but God's creatures. By acting with compassion toward them, however, one is doing so toward the *shekhinah* manifest within them as well.

Dr. Arthur Green was the founding dean and is currently rector of the Rabbinical School at Hebrew College in Newton MA. He is a leading figure of Neo-Hasidism in the contemporary Jewish world, seeking to articulate a contemporary Jewish mysticism, based on the Hasidic model. Dr. Green is author, editor, and translator of over twenty books including Tormented Master: A Life of Rabbi Nahman of Bratslav *and* Radical Judaism. *His most recent work is* Judaism for the World: Reflections on God, Life, and Love *(Yale, 2020).*

Our friend and teacher Rabbi Jonathan Slater has devoted many years of his life to reading and teaching the words of the Hasidic masters. I am proud to have had some small role in encouraging him to do that. Jonathan has always been demanding of his sources as well as of his students. He turns to the Hasidic sources again and again, asking the same question of them that they ask of the Torah text itself. "This text is supposed to be eternal. What does it have to teach us today?" The connection between Hasidut and mussar has been especially close to his heart.

May the Teaching go forward from his generation to the next, as it has from mine to his. May new students and teachers keep turning it over again and again, ever finding new and ancient sparks of divine light within it.

The Fragrance of Torah

Melila Hellner-Eshed

Or Ha-Me'ir is a compilation of Hasidic teachings written by Ze'ev Wolf from Zhitomir. The name given to this book, *Or Ha-Me'ir* "The Light That Shines" seems to me to be a translation into Hebrew of the Zoharic Aramaic term *Nehora d'Nahir*. It is the resplendent light that was created on the first day, then concealed by God. According to the Zohar, this light can be experienced by those who engage lovingly with Torah at night. It shines on those who awaken their consciousness to be able to perceive the great gift of that light. It is also the luminous gift for those who, like the Zoharic *hevraya*, wake up every day before dawn awaiting the *nehora d'nahir*. That shining light fills the world when the king and the gazelle, the blessed holy one and the *Shekhinah*, become one in the fleeting yet redemptive moments of dawn.

Ze'ev Wolf from Zhitomir (d. 1798) was one of the students who sat around the table of the Dov Ber, the great Maggid of Mezritch, disciple of the Ba'al Shem Tov. We know very little about his actual life, but we do have a compilation of homilies he gave on the Torah portions and on the holiday cycle. The book was edited by his disciple Eliezer of Zhitomir.

Ze'ev Wolf did not establish a Hasidic court, as some of the other disciples of the Maggid did in these formative years of the movement. He had a saloon and an inn from which he made his living. He was not an ecstatic, at least not when it came to prayer. Like his master the Maggid, he was a contemplative and an intellectual. Reading through *Or Ha-Me'ir* we find all the major themes that were simmering in the world of the new movement.

I am delighted to offer my reading of one of my favorite teachings of Ze'ev Wolf as a gift of love and deep appreciation to my friend, colleague and teacher of many years, Jonathan Slater, master of Hasidic teachings, a teacher who enlightens the eyes of Israel allowing us to find light in our Torah and to touch those enlivening moments of *Or Ha-Me'ir*.

* * *

The *derashah* opens, closes and interprets throughout, various readings of the verse *"My lover is to me a sachet of myrrh (tzeror ha-mor) resting between my breasts"* (Song 1:13), spoken by the female lover to her beloved. The literal meaning, the *peshat* of the verse relates the way in which the female lover imagines her beloved as a bundle of aromatic fragrant herbs as he lays between her breasts.

Ze'ev Wolf opens his *derashah* with Rashi's commentary to the verse. Following Rabbinic midrash and taking flight on its imagination, Rashi reads the verse as relating to God and the congregation of Israel. Rashi understands it as saying, my beloved (*dodi*), that is, God, has a sachet of myrrh in his bosom, which he gives me, the people of Israel, his beloved. The bundle of myrrh in this reading is of course the Torah. This *midrashic* image of Torah as a perfumed bundle is the portal through which Ze'ev Wolf ventures into a bold teaching.

The verse, says Ze'ev Wolf, describes an ever-present and ever-continuous dynamic. This sachet of myrrh —the Torah—is being given at all times by God to Israel. We know this, he says, by the words we recite after the ritual reading of the Torah, when we bless God as the giver and bestower of Torah. Ze'ev Wolf notes that we say "the one who *gives* us Torah (*notain haTorah* in the present tense) and not, the one who *gave* us the Torah (past tense). God's continuous revelation and ever active giving of the Torah is also present in the verse describing the revelation at Sinai, "The sound of the Shofar goes-*holekh*, a verb that is both present tense and continuous, says Ze'ev Wolf. The divine shofar is forever being sounded throughout the universe. He says that this dynamic revelation and giving of Torah gives rise to the fact that in every generation we find or uncover new combinations and innovations of Torah, for Torah is always being given to us humans.

Ze'ev Wolf then proceeds to develop in a creative way a Rabbinic midrash that interprets the verse about the revelation at Sinai (Ex. 19:19-20) "And then the voice of the shofar sounded louder and louder. Moshe speaks and God answers him in a voice". This verse should be read to mean that Moshe speaks and God answers him in a voice, not a heavenly voice but precisely the voice of Moshe."

Divinity reveals itself in the voice of Moshe, in the human voice that carries in it a human translation and interpretation of revelation.

This early midrash acquired a new level of meaning when the Zohar portrayed *Kol* – voice, as a continuous undifferentiated river of thought, emotion, will and desire and saw it as relating to the distinctly masculine divine quality of the *sefirah Tiferet*. This quality of *kol* is ideally paired with *dibbur*, speech, which takes in voice, breaking up the continuous flow into specific words, carrying a specific meaning and constructing transmittable language. *Dibbur* – speech is seen as a rich symbol of *Shekhinah*, the feminine aspect of divinity.

It is out of love to Israel, says Ze'ev Wolf, that God reveals Torah as undifferentiated sacred sound\voice *kol*. It allows Moshe to put revelation into speech, and for Torah lovers of all future generations, all embodiments of *Shekhinah* and *Knesset Yisrael*, to bring forth their own living *dibbur* out of that *kol*.

Ze'ev Wolf builds on this midrash and relates it not only to Moshe in his time but to any Jewish person in any generation. Each one of us is invited to create their own personal permutation and interpretation of Torah so that Torah will become for us a sachet of myrrh. Our interpretation of Torah ought to become like an aromatic bundle of healing herbs, a Torah that brings comfort and solace to those who engage with her.

The changing needs and life experience of every generation brings the wise ones and leaders of that generation to create new books and innovations in Torah that are alive and relevant. In that way the Torah stays beloved and alive for the people of that generation, and can stay a leading and directing force in their life. Enhancing this image, Ze'ev Wolf quotes a line from a passionate love poem that Rabbi Shimon Bar Yochai, the great hero of the Zohar sings to the Torah. In this poem the Torah appears as the beloved whose breasts satiate her lovers at all times. Adding a radical twist to the Zohar, Ze'ev Wolf stresses that the satiating aspect of Torah is the way she brings forth new interpretations that speak to the values of the time and are attentive to them. The interpretation of Torah is not frozen or static but like voice itself it changes and receives a different meaning in every generation.

Ze'ev Wolf interprets Rashi's commentary as saying that the bundle of myrrh is the Torah given by God in the aspect of voice precisely so as to allow people of each generation to use this voice of infinite range and hues to create new teaching that can comfort their souls.

According to Rashi, the fragrant sachet is God's call to the children of Israel to build the tabernacle which is better for them than the first sachet of myrrh that they lost when they built the golden calf. It seems that in Ze'ev Wolf's reading the first sachet of myrrh that Israel lost are the first tablets, and the Torah given as voice is better for Israel than the first, because of its gift of emitting fragrance in the renewing interpretation of every generation. It is actually the ability to find in Torah relevance to the changing times that brings about the pleasure *oneg* and nourishment that the wise lovers of Torah find in her, and a special *oneg* to God himself.

Ze'ev Wolf ends his Torah with the end of the verse he opened with, *resting between my breasts*. He interprets the breasts as a metaphor to the wise and righteous ones in every generation. The seekers at all times, like babies, massage and press the breasts, the spiritual leaders of their time, seeking for the comforting and life-giving milk **of** Torah. And it is that quest and thirst and probing itself that awakens **those new interpretations**.

God in this teaching consents with love with these new readings of **Torah, and takes pleasure** in the aromatic interpretations addressing the needs of differing times.

Or Ha-Me'ir - Ze'ev Wolf from Zhitomir

A Teaching in Depth: a lesson on Song 1:13

"A bundle of myrrh is my beloved to me, resting between my breasts" (Song 1:13). Rashi comments: My beloved has become for me like one who has a bundle of myrrh at his breast. How shall we understand this? Consider: we recite the Torah blessing, praising God who **"gives** the Torah" [present tense]. This indicates that the blessed Holy One still is giving the Torah, inasmuch as *"the sound of the shofar extends* [i.e., continues]" (Ex. 19:19) even until the coming of our Redeemer!

In each and every generation, teachers add new permutations [of the letters] of the Torah [i.e., new interpretations] that no one ever before had considered.

The blessed Holy One made this possible through wondrous wisdom, giving the Torah as undifferentiated "voice/sound (קוֹל)", as Scripture indicates: "[*Moses speaks]* and God responds to him with a voice/sound" – through

Moses' own voice (Berakhot 45a).

God thus provided that each person would find ease for their soul, creating those permutations that they, alone, are meant to create, deploying the letters of the Torah to which they are connected ... Therefore, so long as one massages Torah, one finds new meanings/ understandings in it to direct their spiritual practice ... That is why new books [interpreting Torah] are published in every generation: they match the generation and its particular spiritual character.

The wise of the generation—according to their understanding of their particular generation—recombine [letters in the] Torah to discern what we are to do. In this vein, we find reported of R. Shimon bar Yochai that he said: "O Torah, Torah, what shall I say of You! You are *a loving doe, a graceful gazelle* (Prov. 5:19) .... *Let her breasts ever quench your thirst*" (Prov. 5:19). Over and over, ever and ever, we can quench our thirst through the delectations of Torah. It teaches us how to serve the Creator according to the time and conditions prevailing now. Torah makes it possible for us to enjoy its instructions.

Against this background, consider our opening verse: *"A bundle of myrrh is my beloved to me"*. The Congregation of Israel praises her Beloved who extended excessive love to her, informing them of the "precious gift [i.e., Torah]" (Avot 3:14) given them: a voice/sound by which they might articulate words, to bring themselves ease for their soul according to their devotions. This is Rashi's profound lesson: "My beloved has become for me like one who has a bag of myrrh at his breast"—this signifies the holy Torah, given from the breast of the blessed Holy One. God then said to me: take this bundle of myrrh; it is given to you eternally, from the time it was given at Sinai throughout the generations, to the coming of our Redeemer, who will give forth Torah (cf. Isa. 51:4). From then to now God says to me: "take this bundle, and let it provide a fragrance even better than the first one you lost".

"Let her breasts ever quench your thirst", according to the

needs of the time you will find in it [i.e., Torah] a new meaning, and a pleasant fragrance. The blessed Holy One strolls through those permutations the wise produce according to the need of the moment.

Thus, we come to conclusion of the verse: *"resting between my breasts"*. Consider this in light of the Sages' teaching: "as with a breast, so long as the infant massages it they find the taste of milk" (Eruvin 54b), so also are the breasts of Torah. Who are they? The *tzaddikim* whose breasts are matured enough to provide for their followers and those who accept their instruction. They constantly adduce new tastes/meanings [in Torah] according to the generation. They can be compared to breasts which can suckle. And the blessed Holy One confirms their teachings. This is the sense of *"resting between my breasts"*.[*]

אור המאיר, זאב וולף מזיטומיר - מורה בעומק שיר השירים
'צְרוֹר הַמֹּר דּוֹדִי לִי בֵּין שָׁדַי יָלִין' (שה"ש א, יג) - ופירש רש"י: דודי נעשה לי כמי שיש לו צרור המור בחיקו, הכוונה כי הנה אנו מברכין [בעליה לתורה] ('ברוך אתה ה') נותן התורה', להורות שהקב"ה נותן עוד את התורה, אשר 'קוֹל הַשֶּׁפַע הוֹלֵךְ' עוד עד ביאת הגואל, בכל דור ודור ודורשיו נתוספים צירופים חדשים בתורה אשר לא שיערו ראשונים.

והכל בחכמה נפלאה עשה הקב"ה, ונתן את התורה בבחינת קול, על שם הכתוב: (שמות יט, יט) "['מֹשֶׁה יְדַבֵּר] וְהָאֱלֹהִים יַעֲנֶנּוּ בְקוֹל' - בקולו של משה" - בכדי שכל אחד מישראל ימצא מרגוע לנפשו, לעשות אותן הצירופים המוטל עליו לצרפם לערך אותיות שיש לו בתורה ... ולכן כל זמן שאדם ממשמש בה מוצא בה טעם חדש לעיקר העבודה המוטל עליו לעשות... ולכן תמצא שכמה ספרים ניתוספים בכל דור ודור, כפי הדור ועניני עובדותיהם, כמו כן ממציאים חכמי הדור צירופים בתורה לדעת מה יעשה ישראל לערך הכרתם של חכמי הדור, ואנו מצינו בזוהר שאמר רשב"י: 'אורייתא אורייתא מה אומר לגבך, אילת אהבים ויעלת חן אנת' .

'דַּדֶּיהָ יְרַוֻּךְ בְכָל עֵת' (משלי ה, יט), כלומר בכל עת ועת ירויון מדשני של תורה, המלמדת לאדם דעת איך לעבוד הבורא לערך העת והזמן הנוהג אז, מרוה להם התורה ליהנות ממנה עצה היעוצה:

* Translated by Jonathan Slater

מול זה בא הרמז 'צְרוֹר הַמֹּר דּוֹדִי לִי' - כנסת ישראל משבחת
לדודה, אשר חיבה יתירה נודעת להם שנתן להם כלי חמדה בבחינת
קול לעשות בחינת דבורים, להמציא מרגוע לנפשם לערך עניני
עבודתם. לזה העמיק רש"י בדבריו הקדושים, דודי נעשה לי כמי
שיש לו צרור המור בחיקו, מורה לתורה הקדושה הניתנה מחיקו
של הקב"ה, ואמר לי, הרי לך צרור המור, זה מסור בידך תמיד מעת
נתינתה במעמד הקדוש עד דור דורים, ועד ביאת הגואל אשר תורה
מאתו תצא (ראה ישעיה נא, ד), ומאז עד אז אמר לי, הרי לך צרור
זה שיתן ריח טוב מן הראשון שאבדת.
ו'יְרַוּוּךְ בְּכָל עֵת' - כפי הצורך מוציא בה טעם חדש וריח טוב,
והקב"ה מטייל באלו הצירופים שחכמי הדור ממציאים לצורך העת,
ולזה גמר אומר הכתוב 'בֵּין שָׁדַי יָלִין' ועל דרך מאמרם מה הדד
הזה כל זמן שהתינוק ממשמש בה מוצא בה טעם חלב, כן שדים
של התורה, הם הצדיקים אשר שדיהם נכונו להניק לעם הנלוים
וסרים למשמעתם, וממציאים בה תמיד לערך הדור טעם חדש והן
המה נקראים בחינת שדים להניק, והקב"ה מסכים על ידם, וזהו
'בֵּין שָׁדַי יָלִין'.

Melila Hellner-Eshed, Ph.D studies and teaches Zohar, researches and writes about zoharic literature and related Jewish studies. She is a senior fellow at the Shalom Hartman institute and has been working with IJS for the past two decades.

She has studied with and from Jonathan over the pas,t decades much Torah, both ancient and new and, as the Zohar loves to say, "ancient-new." He has always sought to find in Torah wisdom and nourishment for our generation. It has been his awe and respect to classical Jewish texts, bound up with his deep attentiveness to our seeking needs, that has brought forth those healing fragrances in his Torah.

Sunrise at Simi Valley
A Tribute to Jonathan Slater

Nehemia Polen

The quiet and verdant campus of Brandeis-Bardin Institute at Simi Valley, California, provided the perfect setting for our IJS clergy leadership winter retreats, focused on inner growth through study of Hasidic texts, mindfulness practice, yoga and silence. The day began with davening—morning prayers. Rather than rote fulfilment of an obligation, davening time was a vehicle for joy, gratitude, communal bonding, and reaching for the Infinite. Each morning service was carefully crafted to honor *keva*—the unfolding sequence of structured prayer, and at the same time channel *kavvanah*—interiority awakened by creative expression. One day, Jonathan and I had planned a sunrise service, for which the entire cohort—over thirty rabbis and cantors—would awaken before dawn, gather together at around 5:30 am, arrange ourselves in single file and ascend a gentle hill whose peak would be the perfect location to await sunrise, at which time we would begin the main portion of the service. The weather was chilly and participants were all bundled in their sweaters, fleeces and windbreakers. We strode up the hill to the accompaniment of a propulsive, jaunty hasidic niggun whose syncopated rhythms helped us shake our tiredness and filled us with vitality. True to our commitment to silence, there was no talking as we walked up the hill, the only sound being the gentle patter of feet and the group's intoning the notes of the niggun.

We reached the hilltop at around 6:00 am, the time for sunrise according to official astronomical tables that we had carefully consulted in our planning. The group took in the beauty of the vista—the rolling hills and lush valleys that surrounded us—and we looked eastward for the rise of the sun. But the sun was nowhere to be seen. 6:10, 6:15, 6:20—I looked at Jonathan and Jonathan looked at me. We were puzzled but gratified that the niggun was continuing—sung with fervor and intensity. No one took out a phone, no one began to chat.

Then, as if by telepathic communication, it hit Jonathan and me simultaneously—sunrise was scheduled for 6:00 AM, but from our elevation it was delayed because the table's calculations were accurate at sea level, while our view was occluded by the Simi Valley foothills. Eventually, of course, the sun did appear, about 7:00 am, with glorious radiance. The best part of this experience, however, was the human response. Rather than show impatience, our retreat participants held fast to their commitment of no talking, no chitchat, no distraction. The niggun *did* continue. Niggun was sacred sound, an offering to God, and therefore not only permitted but very welcome.

Finally, the melody slowed and the dynamics diminished, and eventually we settled into gentle stillness. Our ears continued to reverberate with the niggun's rhythms as we cradled the impress in our shared silence. No one broke the quiet, not one person succumbed to the temptation to make a wry remark, a witty comment. No one tapped screens or checked devices. We gazed with alertness and yearning at the horizon. A verse in Psalms came to mind: My soul waits for the Lord more than those who watch for the morning, more than watchers for the morning (Psalms 130:6).

As we continued to wait for sunrise, something else happened. Our collective gaze was riveted upon the eastern horizon, the place where we knew the sun would eventually appear. But we also began taking in the entire panoramic vista, swiveling our bodies and heads through 360 degrees of mountain terrain. It was then that we noticed something amazing on the *western* horizon—a pillar of multicolor luminescence, similar to a rainbow but ruler-straight and horizontal, without the rainbow's characteristic arc or bow. The horizontal bands of color were vivid and distinct; then they slowly descended and eventually disappeared, melting into the western horizon around the time the sun appeared eastward. Only later in the day, when we had descended the hilltop after davening, did we realize that we had observed the scattering of the sun's rays as viewed from the western sky, opposite the rising sun, a phenomenon called anticrepuscular rays. One of our retreat participants suggested that this is the real meaning of the Mishnaic phrase *amud ha-shachar*, typically translated 'Morning Star' or Venus, but more accurately translated as 'Morning Pillar.'

It was the willingness to hold the container of our presence, to stay in sacred space, that heightened our perception and enabled us to notice the glories of dawn, glories expected and unexpected. Holding sacred space through watchful waiting is what made room for sacred time and sacred activity—melody, verbal prayer, and silence.

This episode exemplifies the very best in mindfulness practice—holding the container, staying focused in the present, trusting one another and the practice itself, supported by the virtues of patience, commitment, and communal solidarity. Jonathan not only teaches these virtues; he lives them and models them for others. This is reminiscent of a *Kedushat Levi* text that we studied together:

...**And the songs of David your servant...**" [from the *Barukh she-amar* benediction that begins the *Pesukei de-Zimra* section of the prayer service]

—the phrase '**the songs of David your servant**' suggests that niggunim *are* sacred service, just like the Temple service of the Levites [the Levites formed choirs whose music accompanied the priestly offerings in the Jerusalem Temple].

That is why the range of musical notes is called "*octave.*"

{Notes separated by an octave have the same letter name and are of the same pitch class, that is—our ears perceive them as the same note but at a higher frequency, actually twice the sound-wave frequency of vibration; and this continues as we move up the scale at ever higher frequencies till the limit of human hearing}

There is always level after level. That is, just as with respect to love of God, there are always higher levels; and so, with reverence for God—levels beyond levels, **so it is with niggunim.** And that is the meaning of *U-veshirei David avdekha*— song is like sacred service; it *is* sacred service—there are always levels beyond levels...

—-Rabbi Levi Yitzhak of Berdichev, *Kedushat Levi Likkutim* (ed. Michael Derbaremdiger, 1997) volume 2, p. 452, s.v. "*U-veshirei David avdekha*"

The implications of this short teaching by Rabbi Levi Yitzhak are manifold. First of all: niggun is more than aesthetic embellishment designed to lend beauty to some other activity; it is sacred service of its own, calling us to higher aspiration, noble vision, altruistic devotion to God, humanity and the cosmos. Furthermore, like every sacred path, the work is never done, never final. Just as there are always deeper levels of reverence and love for God, so are there more resonant modes of internalizing the place that niggun brings us to, more comprehensive inner transformations. And—there are endless new niggunim and new musical styles waiting to be discovered, brought down to this earthly plane!

Our willingness to sing the jaunty niggun many times over, and then to feel the palpable embrace of the silence that followed, allowed the group to attune eyes, ears and spirits ever more clearly, to deepen perceptions of the world and each other, to arrive at a gracious place of compassion and suppleness.

Nehemia Polen is a professor of Jewish Thought at Hebrew College in Newton, MA. He has served with Jonathan on the faculty of the Institute for Jewish Spirituality

Shabbat
In the teaching of the Sefat Emet

Michael Strassfeld

Jonathan and I have been *hevruta* partners for many years, studying a variety of Hasidic texts. The last few years we have been studying the *Sefat Emet*. What is unusual about this book of teachings is that the *Sefat Emet* preached for so many years. He returns again and again to the same verse or midrash in many Torah portions, enabling the reader to see how he elaborates on his earlier teachings or interprets it in a very different way.

In my imagination, he is addressing the Jews of Ger and of neighboring Warsaw. Some are his Hasidim. Some have left the shtetl and its way of life behind and moved to the big city with its modern life of factories and socialism, poverty and wealth. His underlying message is one of encouragement to his followers whether they are in the difficult circumstances of their everyday lives or facing spiritual challenges. For instance, the Sefat Emet teaches that Israel were slaves in Egypt in order to redeem all the sparks in *Mitzrayim*. He implies that *galut/* exile is always an opportunity to effect redemption. (*Pesah TaRMaG inyan ha-omer ve-sefirah*).

In his teachings, he often stresses the possibility for renewal. *Hithadshut/*starting over again is a very frequent theme. In teachings on *parashat ha-hodesh*, he finds the "newness" in the Hebrew word for month. He teaches that each new month brings a possibility of renewal, but especially the month of Nisan because the redemption of Egypt took place in that month and therefore the potential for freedom and renewal is particularly strong each year during Nisan. More strikingly, he understands the line in the Shabbat morning liturgy *ha-mehadesh be-tuvo be-khol yom tamid ma'asei bereishit* to mean every day the world is renewed. Each of us is a *beriah hadashah*—a new being. In fact, the word *tamid/***always** stresses that every moment has the potential for us to be a new person.

What does the *Sefat Emet* mean by renewal? It is seeing the deeper truth of the universe by understanding that creation is the garment that both simultaneously hides and reveals the Divine. Why is renewal possible? Because within each of us is a spark of the divine life force.

שיש בכל לב איש ישראל נקודה טמונה בהתלהבות לה׳ שלא יוכל
להיות נכבה

In a particularly powerful teaching, the *Sefat Emet* states that the spark of holiness cannot be extinguished no matter what we have done. It can always be fanned into a larger flame. (*Tsav TaRMaD*)

Holiness is an assertion that our world contains more than what we can see and touch. He comments frequently that Torah enables us to achieve a way of being that is not limited by the laws of nature (*le-ma'alah mi-derekh ha-teva*). He does not mean that we can do miracles or escape death. He means that there is an added dimension to life— a dimension that can't be seen but can be experienced. In another teaching, he interprets *ein hadash tahat ha-shamesh*, "there is nothing new under heaven" to be true about nature. The laws of nature are immutable, but humans are not limited by nature and can continue to create new things.

For the *Sefat Emet*, Shabbat is a day above nature. It is easier on Shabbat to touch the holy and the Holy one than during the week. He quotes Rashi's comment on Gen. 2:2: What did the world lack at the end of the six days of creation—*menuchah*/rest. The world is completed at the moment that Shabbat begins—*va-yekhulu shamayim va-aretz*/ the heaven and earth were completed. Work is forbidden. He defines *melakhah*/work as humans creating an object like a house. Such creation leads to *peirud*/separation. Creation is something outside of you. Shabbat then is all about unity and oneness. On Shabbat we are to be all *neshamah*/soul. If you do work on Shabbat the separation causes the connection to the *chiyyut*/the life force to be broken which is why the Torah says *me-challeleha mot yumat*—those who violate Shabbat will "die."

Using a word play from the Zohar, he connects *SHaBbaT* with *BoSHeT*. *Boshet* means distress, regret or embarrassment—any of the things that can get in the way of feeling the oneness of Shabbat and its sense of peace and wholeness.

What might the implications of the *Sefat Emet*'s notion of Shabbat be for us?

A traditional Shabbat involves refraining from work and celebrating by eating good food and wearing your best clothes. It may have developed that way because in pre-modern times people worked six days a week and most people engaged in hard physical labor. Having a day of rest and pampering yourself with food and a shabbat nap made perfect sense. However, many of us live in a world of weekends and have a different sense about work, regarding it as a profession rather than just a livelihood. Many of us would rather wear casual clothes to relax than get dressed up on our days off.

Refraining from work is still essential to creating the space for Shabbat to exist, but I was struck by the dichotomy for the Sefat Emet between rest and distress. It seemed to me that as much as working is a violation of Shabbat, being distressed and causing distress would be grave violations as well. Being angry at someone or putting them down would be the definition of the opposite of his vision of unity.

The traditional explanation for covering the Hallah during kiddush, so that the Hallah isn't embarrassed to come second after the wine, no longer seems silly. Central to this notion of Shabbat is a real *shalom bayit*, not one that papers over the problems, but one that encourages us to take not just our money from our pockets but to remove the grievances from our heart on Friday afternoon as part of our *hakhanah/* preparation for Shabbat. You are not allowed to cook on Shabbat and so you need to prepare your meals on Friday, so too you cannot stew your heart in jealousy on Shabbat or see synagogue services as a time to hear or share the latest gossip. *Menuchah* is to first put aside the divisions of the week and then to rest in the oneness of Shabbat which is *me-ein olam haba*—a taste of the world to come.

Each week, I have the *zekhut*/privilege to study with Jonathan the teachings of the *Sefat Emet*. We try to understand what he is teaching and we try to see how we might understand it for today. The simultaneous conversation with the *Sefat Emet* and with Jonathan more times than not leads to a profound new insight into spiritual life. It is a highlight of my week. The teaching below sums it up:

והוא תכלית עבודת האדם. ובכל יום יורד יום הארה חדשה לעובדי
השי״ת כמ״ש ובער כו' הכהן עצים בבוקר בבוקר כו'. והוא שכ'
מחדש בטובו בכל יום. והוא בחי' אהבה שהוא במתנה בחסד עליון.
אכן מזה האור צריך להיות נשאר רשימה בלב כל היום וכל הלילה
לא תכבה.

The purpose of human activity is to keep the flame alive. Everyday a new *he'arah*—insight appears to *ovdei hashem/* those who strive to serve the holy, as it says *baboker baboker*/every morning. And it is written: *hamehadesh be-tuvo be-khol yom*—in God's goodness, God renews the world every day. This is the aspect of love which is a gift of the supernal *hesed*/lovingkindness. Of this light there should be some residue in the heart all day and all night— "a perpetual fire shall be kept burning on the altar, not to be extinguished" (Lev. 6:6).
Sefat Emet Tzav TaRMaZ

Rabbi Michael Strassfeld, the editor of this volume, is rabbi emeritus of the Society for the Advancement of Judaism. His new book, Judaism Disrupted: A Spiritual Manifesto for the 21st Century, *will be published in the spring of 2023 by Ben Yehuda Press.*

Reflections on the weekly Torah portion from *Ben Yehuda Press*

An Angel Called Truth and Other Tales from the Torah by Rabbi Jeremy Gordon and Emma Parlons. Funny, engaging micro-tales for each of the portions of the Torah and one for each of the Jewish festivals as well. These tales are told from the perspective of young people who feature in the Biblical narrative, young people who feature in classic Rabbinic commentary on our Biblical narratives and young people just made up for this book.

Torah & Company: The weekly portion of Torah, accompanied by generous helpings of Mishnah and Gemara, served with discussion questions to spice up your Sabbath Table by Rabbi Judith Z. Abrams. Serve up a rich feast of spiritual discussion from an age-old recipe: One part Torah. Two parts classic Jewish texts. Add conversation. Stir... and enjoy! "A valuable guide for the Shabbat table of every Jew."—Rabbi Burton L. Visotzky, author *Reading the Book*

Torah Journeys: The Inner Path to the Promised Land by Rabbi Shefa Gold shows us how to find blessing, challenge and the opportunity for spiritual transformation in each portion of Torah. An inspiring guide to exploring the landscape of Scripture... and recognizing that landscape as the story of your life. "Deep study and contemplation went into the writing of this work. Reading her Torah teachings one becomes attuned to the voice of the Shekhinah, the feminine aspect of God which brings needed healing to our wounded world." —Rabbib Zalman Schachter-Shalomi

American Torah Toons 2: Fifty-Four Illustrated Commentaries by Lawrence Bush. Deeply personal and provocative artworks responding to each weekly Torah portion. Each two-page spread includes a Torah passage, a paragraph of commentary from both traditional and modern Jewish sources, and a photo-collage that responds to the text with humor, ethical conscience, and both social and self awareness. "What a vexing, funny, offensive, insightful, infuriating, thought-provoking book." —Rabbi David Saperstein

The Comic Torah: Reimagining the Very Good Book. Stand-up comic Aaron Freeman and artist Sharon Rosenzweig reimagine the Torah with provocative humor and irreverent reverence in this hilarious, gorgeous, off-beat graphic version of the Bible's first five books! Each weekly portion gets a two-page spread. Like the original, the Comic Torah is not always suitable for children.

we who desire: poems and Torah riffs by Sue Swartz. From Genesis to Deuteronomy, from Bereshit to Zot Haberacha, from Eden to Gaza, from Eve to Emma Goldman, *we who desire* interweaves the mythic and the mundane as it follows the arc of the Torah with carefully chosen words, astute observations, and deep emotion. "Sue Swartz has used a brilliant, fortified, playful, serious, humanely furious moral imagination, and a poet's love of the music of language, to re-tell the saga of the Bible you thought you knew—and make its implications crystal clear for the life you are right now living." —Alicia Ostriker, author, *For the Love of God: The Bible as an Open Book*

Words for a Dazzling Firmament: Poems/Readings on Bereishit Through Shemot by Abe Mezrich "According to the mystics, the Torah was engraved with black fire on white fire. These poetic midrash too. Read them slowly." —Jay Michaelson, author of *The Gate of Tears: Sadness and the Spiritual Path*

Jewish spirituality and thought from *Ben Yehuda Press*

The Essential Writings of Abraham Isaac Kook. Translated and edited by Rabbi Ben Zion Bokser. This volume of letters, aphorisms and excerpts from essays and other writings provide a wide-ranging perspective on the thought and writing of Rav Kook. With most selections running two or three pages, readers gain a gentle introduction to one of the great Jewish thinkers of the modern era.

Ahron's Heart: Essential Prayers, Teachings and Letters of Ahrele Roth, a Hasidic Reformer. Translated and edited by by Rabbi Zalman Schachter-Shalomi and Rabbi Yair Hillel Goelman. For the first time, the writings of one of the 20th century's most important Hasidic thinkers are made available to a non-Hasidic English audience. Rabbi Ahron "Ahrele" Roth (1894-1944) has a great deal to say to sincere spiritual seekers far beyond his own community.

A Passionate Pacifist: Essential Writings of Aaron Samuel Tamares. Translated and edited by Rabbi Everett Gendler. Rabbi Aaron Samuel Tamares (1869-1931) addresses the timeless issues of ethics, morality, communal morale, and Judaism in relation to the world at large in these essays and sermons, written in Hebrew between 1904 and 1931. "For those who seek a Torah of compassion and pacifism, a Judaism not tied to 19th century political nationalism, and a vision of Jewish spirituality outside of political thinking this book will be essential." –Rabbi Dr. Alan Brill, author, *Thinking God: The Mysticism of Rabbi Zadok of Lublin*

Return to the Place: The Magic, Meditation, and Mystery of Sefer Yetzirah by Rabbi Jill Hammer. A translation of and commentary to an ancient Jewish mystical text that transforms it into a contemporary guide for meditative practice. "A tour de force—at once scholarly, whimsical, deeply poetic, and eminently accessible." —Rabbi Tirzah Firestone, author of *The Receiving: Reclaiming Jewish Women's Wisdom*

Enlightenment by Trial and Error: Ten Years on the Slippery Slopes of Jewish Mysticism, Postmodern Buddhist Meditation, and Heretical Flexidox Spirituality by Rabbi Jay Michaelson. A unique record of the 21st century spiritual search, from the perspective of someone who made plenty of mistakes along the way.

The Tao of Solomon: Finding Joy and Contentment in the Wisdom of Ecclesiastes by Rabbi Rami Shapiro. Rabbi Rami Shapiro unravels the golden philosophical threads of wisdom in the book of Ecclesiastes, reweaving the vibrant book of the Bible into a 21st century tapestry. Shapiro honors the roots of the ancient writing, explores the timeless truth that we are merely a drop in the endless river of time, and reveals a path to finding personal and spiritual fulfillment even as we embrace our impermanent place in the universe.

Embracing Auschwitz: Forging a Vibrant, Life-Affirming Judaism that Takes the Holocaust Seriously by Rabbi Joshua Hammerman.The Judaism of Sinai and the Judaism of Auschwitz are merging, resulting in new visions of Judaism that are only beginning to take shape. "Should be read by every Jew who cares about Judaism." — Rabbi Dr. Irving "Yitz" Greenberg

Institute for Jewish Spirituality authors published by *Ben Yehuda Press*

Eternal Questions by Rabbi Josh Feigelson. In this volume of original essays on the weekly Torah portion, Rabbi Josh Feigelson guides readers on a journey that weaves together Torah, Talmud, Hasidic masters, and a diverse array of writers, poets, musicians, and thinkers. Each essay includes questions for reflection and suggestions for practices to help turn study into more mindful, intentional living.

"This is the wisdom that we always need—but maybe particularly now, more than ever, during these turbulent times."

—Rabbi Danya Ruttenberg, author, *On Repentance and Repair*

Disrupting Judaism: A Spiritual Manifesto for the 21st Century by Rabbi Michael Strassfeld asks: How do you hold on to faith in a modern world? Judaism Disrupted is about the future of Judaism—starting now. Do the time-honored traditions of rabbinic Judaism meet our spiritual needs? Do we feel spiritually sated after a Shabbat service? Is there another way to be a Jew? Rabbi Strassfeld outlines a path that leads to a new Judaism—a new framework with practices that you can start putting into use right away to live a life of meaning with a revitalized Judaism.

"A clear-eyed statement of what Jewish life can and should be for a meaningful, livable future, beyond mitzvah to commitment, joy, social-justice, and love. May we all embrace such disruption." —Rabbi Jonathan Slater, author, *Mindful Jewish Living: Compassionate Practice*

Torah Journeys: The Inner Path to the Promised Land by Rabbi Shefa Gold shows us how to find blessing, challenge and the opportunity for spiritual transformation in each portion of Torah. An inspiring guide to exploring the landscape of Scripture... and recognizing that landscape as the story of your life.

"Deep study and contemplation went into the writing of this work. Reading her Torah teachings one becomes attuned to the voice of the Shekhinah, the feminine aspect of God which brings needed healing to our wounded world."

—Rabbib Zalman Schachter-Shalomi

In the Fever of Love by Rabbi Shefa Gold breathes new life into the ancient practice of both Jews and Christians to read the Song as an allegory of the love between God and human beings. Rather than address herself to the reader, Rabbi Gold speaks directly, and passionately, to God, The Beloved. She invites us to share in her conversation with life itself.

"A daring and original commentary." —Rabbi Arthur Green

Are We There Yet by Rabbi Shefa Gold turns travel into a spiritual practice. Rabbi Gold shares her experience and insight on travel and helps us reexamine our natural inclination to focus on our destinations—both physical and spiritual. Ride along with her on her many journeys—some mundane, some mysterious, and a few near miraculous—and discover the joy of what can happen when you stop worrying about there and focus on here.

"This is Rabbi Shefa at her quintessential, charismatic best: tour guide to life itself demonstrating how every moment can open into discovery, awakening, revelation." —Sylvia Boorstein, author of *That's Funny, You Don't Look Buddhist: On Being a Faithful Jew and a Passionate Buddhist*

CPSIA information can be obtained
at www.ICGtesting.com
Printed in the USA
JSHW020144041222
34308JS00001B/5